Jan. 18, 2012

OLDEST CHICAGO

DAVID ANTHONY WITTER

FIRST EDITION

www.lakeclaremont.com
Chicago

Oldest Chicago
David Anthony Witter

Published January 2011 by:

LAKE CLAREMONT PRESS

lcp@lakeclaremont.com
www.lakeclaremont.com

Publisher's Cataloging-In-Publication Data
(Prepared by The Donohue Group, Inc.)

Witter, David Anthony.
    Oldest Chicago / David Anthony Witter. -- 1st ed.

        p. : ill. ; cm.

    Includes bibliographical references and index.
    ISBN: 978-1-893121-44-7

        1. Chicago (Ill.)--Description and travel. 2. Historic sites--Illinois--Chicago--Guidebooks. 3. Business enterprises--Illinois--Chicago--History. 4. Chicago (Ill.)--Buildings, structures, etc.--Guidebooks. I. Title.

F548.18 .W58 2010
917.7311 / 04   2009930765

Publisher's Credits
Cover design by Timothy Kocher. Interior design and layout by Charisse Antonopoulos. Editing by June Sawyers, Sharon Woodhouse, Therese Newman, and Becky Straple. Proofreading by Sharon Woodhouse, Becky Straple, and Ken Woodhouse. Indexing by Rachael Patrick and Ken Woodhouse.

CONTENTS

II. FOOD, FUN, AND ENTERTAINMENT

III. THE SUBURBS AND EXURBS

INTRODUCTION

For those who grew up in Chicagoland there was always one magical place—a bakery you went to with your brothers and sisters, a house you drove by on foggy nights, an ice cream parlor that your parents took you to, a restaurant where your grandparents ate their favorite ethnic foods—that survived the passage of time. Over the years, the place might have become a little more run-down. Maybe the sign was broken, or the original owners were no longer standing behind the counter. Still, returning to this place gave you a sense of continuity and tradition in an ever-changing world. These places are disappearing.

Chicago's successes are due to its ability to reconstruct itself. After the Chicago Fire reduced the city to a pile of rubble in

1871, Chicagoans immediately began rebuilding, and they never stopped. A sophisticated street grid, brick mansions, and the world's first skyscrapers replaced plank sidewalks and shacks. The steel mills belching fire and smoke, the stockyards with their rivers of blood, and the waste-producing manufacturing plants receded for the clean efficiency of financial markets, banks, and service industry headquarters. The nation's largest railroad system gave way to the world's busiest airport. The hand-cut stone and ornate terra cotta structures of many of Chicago's great movie palaces flattened for mall movie houses. Larger, taller glass-and-steel structures replaced many of the first stone skyscrapers. In a massive gentrification project over the last twenty years, thousands of frame and tarpaper houses fell in favor of multi-unit, brick-and-cinder-block condominiums. Small, mom-and-pop stores, taverns, coffeehouses, and burger joints are becoming harder to find and new franchises fill the neighborhoods.

Rather than celebrate and preserve the past, Chicago's industrialists and civic leaders have risen to power by tearing it down. In many ways, this has been beneficial. The phrase "rust belt" associated with Cleveland, Gary, Buffalo, and Detroit does not apply to the Windy City. However, Chicago has lost, and continues to lose, many great civic, architectural, and cultural landmarks.

Take, for example, the Tivoli Theater. Located at 63rd Street and Cottage Grove Avenue, the theater boasted a solid marble lobby, terra cotta porticos, three-story high velvet curtains, and chandeliers modeled after the palace of Versailles. It was built in 1921 and destroyed in the 1960s. Another performance center, the Schiller/Garrick Theater, designed by Dankmar Adler and Louis Sullivan, featured a theater space seven stories high, topped by offices that were once leased by the likes of Frank Lloyd Wright. It was demolished to make way for a parking garage. Chicago's losses include Potter Palmer's Castle, the Granada Theater, the Century Theater, the Coliseum, and so many others—all torn down to make way for high-rises, senior citizen homes, shopping malls, and housing developments.

The demise of these structures and other noteworthy businesses are detailed in the press, railed against by neighborhood groups, or protested by architectural commissions. But what about the smaller neighborhood gems and local businesses? Places like the Buffalo Ice Cream Parlor, Lockwood Castle, Rocky's Fish on Navy Pier, and the Parkway Theater are no less worthy of our attention. These and hundreds of other neighborhood bars, restaurants, and eclectic shops that make up the heart and soul of Chicago are vanishing.

This book celebrates the structures that have endured. Some are famous monuments or natural sites that will remain for many decades to come. Some are small businesses that may not. Through the will of a family, a neighborhood, a group of customers, or a historical society, these places are still here. This book aims to aid in the preservation of Chicago's identity and sense of home.

I hope that as you read this book you will discover the magic of these places. Their walls have seen the change from horses to streetcars to busses and cars. Their products and services have been enjoyed by gangsters, soldiers, hippies, and yuppies. By walking in their doorways and listening to their owners' stories, the history of Chicago comes alive, transforming time if only long enough for you to drink a beer, eat an ice cream cone, or gaze out a window. It is my great wish that while reading this book you will take the time to visit these living vestiges of living Chicago history and help maintain these gems for a younger generation.

To paraphrase Langston Hughes, you must not only read and talk about these marvelous structures, you must support them. Go to that famous old restaurant, bar, theater, or other establishment. Pull out your dollars, swipe your credit cards, and open your checkbook. Support local preservation societies. Attend meetings, fundraisers, and benefits. Spread the word about these places and their terra cotta façades, old world recipes, and glowing neon signs. If not, our region may become like so much of modern America, filled with prefabricated construction, recipes altered by chemists, and gigantic plastic signs emitting the still, florescent image of a giant hamburger, donut, or taco, shining 24/7 down your street and into your bedroom window.

1. The 1800s Club

OLDEST CHURCH

FIRST UNITED METHODIST CHURCH
77 W. Washington Street
(1831)

The Reverend Jesse Walker was a famous Methodist circuit rider, spreading the gospel across the Midwest on horseback. Jesse "the Daniel Boone of Methodism" Walker worked as a missionary to the Potawatomi tribe in the 1820s. Then, in 1831, Walker and Rev. Stephen R. Beggs rode to Fort Dearborn. The next day they began to convert Chicago's earliest settlers.

"Our church began in a log cabin, the home of a blacksmith, William See, and his wife Minerva. With Beggs preaching and Walker exhorting, eight people joined the church that day, and the oldest church in Chicago was born," writes Roy Larsen, co-author of the booklet, *Born in a Log Cabin/Alive at 175.*

The cabin stood near the intersection of the north and south branches of the Chicago River. It wasn't far from Miller's Tavern and the Sauganash Hotel, spots where traders swindled valuable items from Native Americans, gambled, drank, fought, and caroused. Today, the area is known as "the cradle of Chicago," but in 1833, an English visitor named Joseph Latrobe described the area in less than charitable terms: "The interior of the village was a chaos of mud, rubbish and confusion," he wrote.

One year after the city was incorporated, the preaching of Rev. Peter Boren inspired three hundred people, or one-tenth of the city's current population, to join the church. Boren's words also spurred church members to seek a location away from the river and the unsavory places nearby. In 1838 parishioners rolled the log cabin church to the river, barged it across, and then set it down at Washington and Clark streets. Now over 175 years later the Methodist congregation is still meeting on almost that very spot.

In 1845, First United Methodist Church moved out of the log cabin and into a brick-and-mortar church. Chicago's seventh mayor and regular church member, Augustus Garrett, dedicated the new building. With a spire, sanctuary, clock tower, and belfry, the new church was very different from the log cabin surrounded by swamp.

In 1851, the church was instrumental in establishing the first of many Methodist-based institutions in the area, Northwestern University. As the 1860s approached, the members of the church also played a small but important role in the abolitionist movement. Chicago historian A. T. Andreas transcribed a report by Elizabeth Marquardt and John Knight that described how "an escaped former slave was invited to address a meeting at the church." Apparently, not all of the church members were happy with this, and some doused the lights while "the former slave continued his speech in a calm voice until he was finished."

In 1871 the Great Chicago Fire burned most of the young city, including the first church, to the ground. While the ashes of the fire were still smoldering, Briggs, then 88 years old, stated: "I have seen Chicago come up from the beginning and burn down and rebuilt in every aspect greater than before. It is an utter impossibility to burn pluck, courage, and faith—they are the indestructible gifts of God." While many members urged the church to rebuild in another location, it remained in downtown Chicago.

Throughout the years, many important figures in the history of Chicago's religious and charitable community have passed through the doors of First United Methodist Church. These include Dwight L. Moody (of the Moody Bible institute and YMCA), Frances E. Willard (suffragist and leader of the Woman's Christian Temperance Union), and Lucy Rider Meyer (philanthropist).

In 1924, the congregation's fifth church building was dedicated. A magnificent spire, it was the tallest edifice in Chicago at the time. It today stands in the center of a teeming metropolis, surrounded by the financial district to the west, the shopping district to the east, and the Civic Center and Daley Plaza across the street to the north. If the word, image, and spirit of the gospel inside the church are not enough to inspire the congregation, the works of two of the world's most famous artists, Pablo Picasso and Joan Miró, are just yards away.

The church also contains its own artistic masterworks, including stained glass work detailing the life of Jesus according to the apostles Mathew, Mark, Luke, and John, as well as 17 more stained glass windows depicting scenes from the Bible. In 1965, ten more stained glass panels were added. They depict the white and Native American traders, the first log cabin church, Rev. Jesse Walker, the Chicago Fire, and the five First United Methodist Church and Chicago Temple structures that have been a part of the city of Chicago since its first days.

People often say that a church is the heart and soul of a community. This church has been part of Chicago since the days when Native Americans paddled their canoes up the Chicago River to trade with the white men. Although they may not be as celebrated as famous buildings or sculptures, the worshippers in congregations, parishes, churches, and temples helped to make the city of Chicago what it is today.

Visit this beautiful church at 77 West Washington Street. The church holds services Wednesday, Thursday, Friday, Saturday, and Sunday. They also offer numerous volunteer opportunities. View their website at www.chicagotemple.org for more information.

☞ ITS STAINED GLASS WINDOWS AND GOTHic woodwork help make the First United Methodist Church a welcome sanctuary of peace and quiet amidst the bustle of downtown Chicago. It is indeed a marvel that this temple of worship and peace has survived for over 175 years in the heart of Chicago's Loop. In the plaza just east of the church is the **Miro's Chicago** (1981) sculpture; across Washington Street in Daley Plaza is the more famous untitled **Chicago Picasso** (1967). The landmark **City Hall–County Building** also sits on this square—the county has the east half of the structure (enter on Clark Street); the city has the west side (a La Salle Street address). Next to that on the northwest corner of Clark and Randolph streets is Helmut Jahn's **State of Illinois building** (now known as the Thompson Center), another architectural wonder to check out, also with a piece by a famous sculptor out front: Jean Dubuffet's **Monument With Standing Beast** (1984).

OLDEST HOUSE

CLARKE HOUSE
1827 S. Indiana Avenue
(1836)

The Clarke House is not only Chicago's oldest house, but it is older than the city itself. In 1836, one year before the city was incorporated, Henry Clarke and his wife, Caroline, traveled from upstate New York to Chicago. It was little more than a swamp surrounded by prairie, but Clarke saw opportunity there.

He began constructing a Greek Revivalist home at what is now 16th Street and Michigan Avenue. The large portico frame, Roman Doric columns, and Italianate cupola give the home the look of a smaller, midwestern version of Jefferson's Monticello. In her earliest letters, Mrs. Clarke wrote that she could see and smell the campfires of the Native Americans as the house was being built. At a time when most Chicago homes were log cabins, writer James McConkey described Greek Revival homes as "a dream of order, balance and proportion set down in the rude wilderness."

With the rest of the money he had saved as a dry goods salesman in New York, Clarke started a business. "Clarke opened Chicago's first bank, the Second Bank of Illinois," Edward Maldonado, curator of the Clarke House Museum, states. "But then the country went back to the gold standard. There was an economic panic in 1837 and Henry Clarke lost all of his money. Because of this, the interior of the home went unfinished."

Clarke tried to reinvent himself. Going into politics, he became a city clerk. Today, the job is a political plum; the sale of city automobile stickers and licensing fees bring in hundreds of millions of dollars. There was little to license in the 1840s, however, and Clarke was forced to support his family through hunting and trapping. Things got even worse. In 1849, Clarke died in one of the city's many cholera epidemics, and the Clarke House, now part of the city of Chicago and subject to its taxes, remained unfinished.

"The true story of the Clarke House and its survival really began after Henry Clarke died in 1849," Maldonado aserts. "It is not only the story of the survival of a home, but the story of women in the nineteenth century. Somehow, Mrs. Clarke was not only able to keep the house, but she was actually responsible for finishing it and even updating it to what was the changing architectural and social styles of the time. It was phenomenal how she was able to keep up appearances for so many years. Towards the end of her life she even hinted at the possible historical significance that the home might have."

In 1871, the Great Chicago Fire raged through the city, destroying many of Chicago's earliest commercial and residential structures. Because of its southern location, the Clarke House was one of the few wooden structures to survive the catastrophe.

In 1872, the Clarke children sold the house to John Chrimes. Wary of another fire and the problems with sewage and sanitation that were responsible for the cholera epidemics and the original homeowner's death, Chrimes moved the house to 45th Street and Wabash Avenue. "The house was jacked up, put on logs, then rolled on a long flatbed pulled by horses and mules," Maldonado says. "Since there were no real roads leading there, it must have been a difficult task." The house remained in what was then countryside, a quiet and uneventful area. It remained in the Chrimes family for the next sixty years.

In 1941, his granddaughters sold the house to Bishop Henry Louis Ford, who used it as a parish hall, parsonage, and community center until 1977. "In 1977 Ford wanted to build a more modern church," Maldonado explains. "He was an important figure in the black community and saw that he could get a better price by selling it to the city. In the 1930s, the Works Project Administration conducted a survey on historical homes, known as the HABS project, which documented the Clarke House as having historical value. Based on this evidence, Ford convinced the City of Chicago to buy the home in 1977."

At that time, the city was in the beginning stages of making the old Prairie Avenue area a historical district and, since that area was close to the original location of the home, moving the home seemed a natural fit. If the first move through woodland and brush seemed difficult, it was nothing compared to the problems with moving the house through the city in the 1970s. "They not only had the Dan Ryan Expressway, but the CTA elevated train tracks to negotiate," Maldonado says. "The Dan Ryan was avoided when the train was taken via flatbed truck down Lake Shore Drive. But it had to be jacked up, put on steel girders, then shot like a sled in order to get up, over, and down the 'L' tracks. This was in December and some of the hydraulic equipment froze. So the house had to sit on jacks above the 'L' tracks for two weeks until the weather thawed."

The home was restored by the City of Chicago in 1980. In 2004, photos were found of the house and parts of it were once again reconstructed in order to fit the house's original appearance more accurately. Today, the Department of Cultural Affairs and the National Society of Colonial Dames uses the Clarke house as a museum. Tours of the Clarke House and nearby Glessner House are given Wednesday through Sunday at noon, one, and two. The Clarke House is located at 1827 South Indiana Avenue. Call 312/326-1480 for reservations.

☞ THE PRAIRIE AVENUE HISTORICAL DISTRICT is on the National Register of Historic Places. Chicago's greatest industrialists including George Pullman, Marshall Field, Philip Armour, and Joseph Sears all lived there during the late 1800s. Time and the wrecking ball have, unfortunately, put an end to most of these great mansions. Besides the Clarke House, the John J. Glessner House and Museum is the only major structure left unaltered from the neighborhood's glory days.

Throughout the 1960s, 70s, and 80s, the area around the Clarke House was basically a no-man's land, consisting largely of abandoned houses, shuttered storefronts, and empty warehouses. The restoration and moving of the Clarke House, and the designation of the 1800–1900 blocks of South Prairie as a city landmark in 1979, began to change this. Thirty years later not only Prairie Avenue, but the entire area, is a thriving, urban neighborhood filled with newly developed million-dollar townhomes, as well as bars, restaurants, and shops. The developers have, by and large, honored the area's history, with elements such as copper roofs and gutters, ornate windows, wrought iron balconies, and other features which lend themselves to the area's historic theme, adorning new structures.

The anchor of all this is still the Clarke House, and the **John J. Glessner House and Museum** (1800 S. Prairie Ave., 312/326-1397). This 27-room mansion designed by architect Henry Hobson Richardson features tours, a gift shop, and even frequent dramatic readings and performances. Tours are given Wednesday through Sunday at 1:00 PM and 3:00 PM **The National Vietnam Veterans Art Museum** (1801 S. Indiana Ave., 312/326-0270), exhibiting art by Vietnam Veterans, is just a block west. Two blocks south and two blocks west is **Willie Dixon's Blues Heaven Foundation** and museum (2120 S. Michigan Ave., 312/808-1286), the former home of the Chess Records label. It is here that Muddy Waters, Chuck Berry, and even The Rolling Stones recorded the songs that helped create what is now rock and roll. Jazz fans can hear live jazz at innovative jazzman Fred Anderson's place, the **New Velvet Lounge** (67 E. Cermak Rd., 312/791-9050).

Finally, one can't ignore the host of new restaurants in this area. The most interesting of these may be the **Chicago Firehouse Restaurant** (1401 S. Michigan Ave., 312/786-1401). Formerly a turn of the century Chicago Fire Department firehouse, it has been elegantly restored into a casual upscale eatery.

C.D. PEACOCK JEWELERS
(1837)

In 1837, downtown Chicago was little more than a few shacks, primitive buildings, and paths built over swamps. The city had a population of 4,100 people and had just elected William Ogden as its first mayor. The area outside of the two-and-a-half-square-mile town was mostly prairie or farmland. Fort Dearborn had closed within the same year and the Potawatomi still occupied much of the land on what is now the city's far Northwest Side. It was during this year that Elijah Peacock of Peacock Jewelers began buying, selling, and trading gemstones in a small building on Lake Street. Peacock Jewelers is, easily, *Chicago's oldest.*

Elijah Peacock was a silversmith and a watch and jewelry repairman. Peacock's skill at repairing watches was said to have

added to the efficiency and speed of Chicago's business community. Peacock also added a touch of class. "After the House
of Peacock opened in 1937, he started to introduce the kinds
of things that distinguished Chicago as a true city," Dean Walter, operations manager and marketing director for C.D. Peacock's Oakbrook store, says. He presented English tea service,
handcrafted and engraved sterling silver coffee trays, tea sets,
and candlesticks to Chicago's growing merchant class. Most of
these businessmen and their wives had come to Chicago from
the East, and were eager to bring some of the known luxuries
to "the Wild West." Locals heralded the opening of the city's
first retail jewelry store as a sign that Chicago had passed "from
semi-savage conditions to civilization and refinement."

The House of Peacock remained on Lake Street until 1849.
Businessmen such as Charles Wacker and Marshall Field started
to settle what was to be Chicago's main merchandizing area
south and east towards what is now the Loop (the term "Loop"
was not used until the 'L' trains were installed in the 1890s), and
Peacock was asked to move his establishment there as well. Early customers at Peacock's new store included Chicago's wealthiest and most prominent citizens. These included Cyrus McCormick, Potter Palmer, Marshall Field, George Pullman, and Mary
Todd Lincoln.

It remained on Randolph Street until 1871, the year of the
Chicago Fire. Just as Peacock had foreseen the development of
Chicago, he was also cognizant of the danger of fire. Accord-
ingly, he locked all of his valuable merchandize in a fireproof
vault, and in 1873 the business re-opened. "During this time the
father began to pass the business on to his son Charles Daniel,
and in 1889 the name was officially changed to C.D. Peacock,"
Walter says.

In 1896, the business moved to State and Washington, where
it remained until 1927. During that year, it moved across the

street to the Palmer House hotel at the intersection of State and Monroe. Many Chicagoans are still familiar with the ornately sculptured bronze doors at the State and Monroe location, sculpted in the shape of flowing peacocks. Inside, mahogany counters, Tiffany chandeliers, and Verde Antico Marble decorated the store. Treasures for sale included diamonds, precious and semi-precious gemstones, pearls, platinum, gold, sterling silver, watches, fine crystal, porcelain, china, enamels, silver, and collectables from around the world. The most famous of these was the Peacock Diamond, a flag yellow diamond weighing 21.81 carats and mounted in 18k platinum and gold, which cost $495,000.

For decades, Chicagoans of wealth and moderate means bought their jewelry for engagements, weddings, and anniversaries at C.D. Peacock. Celebrities, athletes, and dignitaries from around the world also purchased their jewelry there. During the 1960s long-haired rock and roll legend Mick Jagger strode into C.D. Peacock. With his *Get Your Ya's Out* get-ups that often featured top hats and tails, he would have fit right in with the fashions worn by the Palmers, Fields, and Pullmans a century before.

In the 1980s, Canadian jewelry baron Henry Birks purchased the store. At that time the Loop was in decline, and Birks moved the flagship store out of the Palmer House and opened a string of C.D. Peacock stores in suburban shopping centers in La Grange, Aurora, and Skokie (Old Orchard). "He wanted to have a presence in the United States, and purchased C.D. Peacock, as well as jewelry stores like Caldwells in Michigan," Walter says. "He later put his three sons in as managers, and opened a bunch of stores in lots of places. But Birks got into trouble and went bankrupt. He didn't sell off C.D. Peacock but reduced it to just one store."

In the early 1990s, C.D. Peacock was purchased by current owner Seymour Holtzman, who opened a store in Northbrook in 1998 and later a store in Oakbrook. Today the C.D. Peacock name is carried on in stores at 520 North Michigan Avenue and 342 North Michigan Avenue in Chicago, Northbrook Court in Northbrook, Oakbrook Center in Oak Brook, and Woodfield Mall in Schaumburg.

IF YOU ARE STILL IN THE MOOD FOR HIGH-end, old-fashioned elegance, walk or take your limo four blocks north to **Truefitt and Hill** (900 N. Michigan Ave., Level 6, 312/337-2525), Chicago's most elegant barbershop. The original Truefitt and Hill was founded in London in 1805. Barbers at the London location have administered shaves and/or haircuts to the likes of Winston Churchill, Charles Dickens, Prince Charles, Prince Phillip, Fred Astaire, Cary Grant, and Alfred Hitchcock. The Chicago locale has not served royalty, but it still offers service fit for a king. Paneled with 120-year-old mahogany, the décor is old English gentleman, with pictures of race horses, hunting dogs, and wooded hunting scenes gracing the walls. Services include old-fashioned, hand heated and lathered straight razor shaves, haircuts, massages, manicures, and related rituals for the discerning gentleman. The price is higher than your average corner barber—a total package with a one-hour body massage, hot lather shave, haircut, manicure, pedicure, and shoe shine runs $270. But a haircut alone costs about $55, not that much higher and even lower than many boutiques.

OLDEST PARK

WASHINGTON SQUARE PARK/ BUGHOUSE SQUARE
Dearborn, Walton, and Clark streets
(1843)

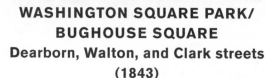

While Chicago boasts the lakefront, a large park system, and the Cook County Forest Preserves, Washington Square Park is one of the city's few public squares. The park originated in 1842, when the city received a three-acre parcel from the American Land Company. The city decorated the former cow pasture with a fountain, fencing, benches, and traditional diagonal footpaths leading towards the centerpiece. A new black iron fountain of simple design surrounded by a wrought iron fence was added in the early 1900s. It resembles the fountains of town squares in New Orleans and Savannah.

Washington Square Park soon became Chicago's free-speech center. "People would bring their own soap boxes or platforms to stand on, and read political oratories, recite poems, sing songs, or just rant on any subject upon which they were compelled to speak," Richard Brown of the Newberry Library says. "It appealed to communists, labor organizers, artists, poets, songwriters, bohemians, and radicals—anyone who had something different to say."

Some of the more famous regulars at the square included Ben "the Clap Doctor" Reitman, Frederick "the Sirfessor" Wilkesbarr, Herbert "the Cosmic Kid" Shaw, and Marxist-feminist Martha Biegler. In later years, author and famed Chicago historian Studs Terkel was also a regular attendee and participant in events at Bughouse Square. Bughouse Square remained a popular forum through the 1950s and 1960s, when it became a center for Beatnik poets and the early days of the anti–Vietnam War movement.

"Bughouse Square began to die down during the late 1960s," Brown says. "There were a lot of reasons for its demise, but it was probably television that killed it."

The park is surrounded by the impressive, brownstone structure of the Newberry Library, new town homes along Clark Street, and a wall of high-rises along Dearborn and Walton streets. Lined with shady trees, benches, and often featuring a statue or a fountain in the center, public squares offer city dwellers a refuge from the noise and hustle of the city.

Today, office workers on lunch breaks, afternoon strollers, condominium dwellers, and dog walkers frequent the park more than radicals and activists. In 1991, the park was added to the U.S. National Register of Historic Places and designated a Chicago landmark. Even if you do not live in the area, take a sandwich or cup of your favorite coffee, watch the people, feed the squirrels, and enjoy this urban treasure.

WASHINGTON SQUARE PARK IS LOCATED across the street from the **Newberry Library** (see Oldest Reference Library, p. 90) in the heart of the Near North Side. Nearby attractions include **Loyola University's downtown campus** (820 N. Michigan Ave.), as well as neighborhood favorites like the 24-hour **Tempo Restaurant** (6 E. Chestnut St., 312/943-4373) and **Potash Brothers**, one of the cities oldest family-owned grocery stores (875 N. State St., 312/266-4200). Originally opened in 1950 as Pleezing Foods, Potash Brothers combines the look and feel of a store from a 1960s TV show with a full-service gourmet deli and wine shop. Now in its third generation, it is the oldest family-owned business in the area. Other sites of interest are the **Chicago Water Tower** (see Oldest Public Building, p. 35), the **Water Tower Place** shopping center (835 N. Michigan Ave.), and the **John Hancock Center** (875 N. Michigan Ave.). Otherwise, this high-traffic and high-income area is in a constant state of demolition and rebuilding. The **Chestnut Street Theaters** (830 N. Clark St.), once housed in an art deco building that was formerly a post office, were closed in 1999. The **Esquire Theater** (58 E. Oak St.) also has an appointment with the wrecking ball. Yet Washington Park Square endures, a place where seniors congregate, those in corporate attire scurry by, and modern-day Holly Golightlys walk their dogs, smoke, read, and display the latest in fashion.

CHICAGO TRIBUNE
435 N. Michigan Avenue
(1847)

"Extra Extra, Read All About It!" seems like a quaint phrase from the movies—and it is. But there was a time when there were over a dozen major newspapers in the city of Chicago and a newsstand or newsboy competing on every corner.

The *Chicago Tribune* began in 1847, with a run of four hundred copies, in a one-room office at the intersection of Lake Street and Madison Avenue. Joseph Medill and Colonel Robert McCormick are responsible for turning it into the media giant that it is today. Medill was an abolitionist and early supporter of Abraham Lincoln, and one of early Chicago's most enthusiastic proponents. McCormick was also a great supporter of Chicago. After the Chicago Fire demolished much of the city, including the *Tribune* plant at Dearborn and Madison streets, the *Tribune* published the famous headline, "Chicago Shall Rise Again." Medill's boosterism led to him being elected mayor of Chicago, and during his term, the city rebuilt itself.

Medill was succeeded by two of his grandsons, Joseph Medill Patterson and Robert R. McCormick. Colonel Robert R. McCormick (known as such for of his service in World War I) became a legend in the journalism business. Readers knew McCormick for his unique way of spelling. He often shortened words by dropping their silent letters: *definit* (definite), *patroled* (patrolled), and *analog* (analogue). Colonel McCormick ran the newspaper for almost half of a century. During his reign, the Chicago Tribune built the immense, gothic Tribune Tower at 435 North Michigan Avenue, which is now a Chicago landmark. McCormick also helped to establish wGN radio in 1924 and wGN television in 1948.

Although McCormick will be remembered for his great contributions to journalism and broadcasting, McCormick and the *Chicago Tribune* were also responsible for one of the greatest mistakes in journalism history. The headline "Dewey Defeats Truman" was printed before the full results of the 1948 presidential election were tabulated. When the results came in, Harry S Truman won the election. President Truman mockingly held up the *Chicago Tribune* the morning after the election and the photo was printed in newspapers across the nation.

In recent years the newspaper has continued to expand into various media markets. In 2007 the company was purchased by real estate magnate Sam Zell.

☞ JUST STEPS FROM THE TRIBUNE BUILDING is a staircase at Michigan Avenue and the Chicago River that leads to one of Chicago's most magnificent attractions, a Chicago River cruise with **Wendella Boats** (www.wendellaboats.com), the oldest tour boat company on the river. Operated by the Borgstrom family since 1935, Wendella is also one of the city's oldest family-run businesses. Take your pick from the Chicago River Architecture Tour, a lake/river cruise, a sunset cruise, a quick water taxi ride, and even fireworks and wine tasting cruises, among other specialty offerings.

OLDEST CEMETERY

OAK WOODS CEMETERY
1065 E. 67th Street
(1852)

 ak Woods Cemetery not only reveals the racial strife and advances in race relations central in Chicago history, it may also represent the wide and varied history of Chicago as much as any location in the city.

This 183-acre site is the final resting place for a good portion of the city's most celebrated and infamous citizens. Many major players in religion, politics, sports, science, music, and crime are spending eternity here, including many of the city's great African-American leaders, athletes, and artists.

Some may cite irony, others will cite history, but just a short walk from the graves of many prominent black Chicagoans is the Confederate Mound Monument. Erected in 1893, the monument is the mass burial site for over six thousand Confederate soldiers and sailors who died at Camp Douglas, which was located near Lake Michigan about five miles north of Oak Woods. At one time, it was the largest Confederate prison camp in the North. Camp Douglas was a crowded hell hole, where prisoners were not only subjected to the brutal Chicago weather but also rampant dysentery, disease, and cruel treatment from guards who denied prisoners food and clothing. In a particularly brutal four-month winter span, the camp lost over one thousand prisoners. The monument to these fallen men marks the largest burial ground for Confederate soldiers north of the Mason–Dixon Line, and the largest mass grave in the Western Hemisphere. Placed on the east end of a large lagoon, the monument consists of a two-story-high pillar upon which stands a statue of a weary Confederate soldier. At the base of the statue are reliefs depicting the conditions of the camp; beneath this are nearly six hundred names of fallen Confederate prisoners cast in bronze. Surrounding the monument are four Confederate cannons, in front of which cannon balls are placed in neat, triangular piles.

The monument could have been taken from any town square in Tennessee, but it stands in Chicago. Even more paradoxical is the graves of so many African-American leaders that are within a short walk. The following are just a few of the more important figures whose final resting place is Oak Woods:

⇨ Harold Washington: State senator, U.S. Congressman, the first black mayor of Chicago. Many say his political tactics and reliance on community organization helped to inspire the campaign of President Barack Obama.

⇨ Jesse Owens: Olympic Gold Medalist who defeated Hitler's Nazi athletes in the 1936 Olympics in Berlin. It may have been the first time many white Americans openly cheered for a black man.

⇨ Ida B. Wells: Political reformer and community organizer who ranks as one of the most prominent African-American women in Chicago's history (before Oprah).

Other prominent black leaders interred at Oak Woods include: John H. Johnson, founder of *Ebony* and *Jet* magazines; Cecil Partee, former states attorney and Chairman of the Illinois State Senate; and Eugene Sawyer, the second black mayor of Chicago who succeeded Washington. There's also a designated final resting place for former Illinois attorney general and U. S. senator Roland Burris. Many African-American musicians are also buried at Oak Woods, including Thomas A. Dorsey, the father of modern gospel music; "Little Brother" Montgomery, a piano player who migrated from New Orleans to Chicago not long after Louis Armstrong and whose career spanned the eras of Dixieland, boogie woogie, and Chicago blues; Roebuck "Pops" Staples, patriarch of the Staples Singers; and Junior Wells, a man who combined Delta blues with funk and soul, and became known as one of the greatest harmonica players in all of blues.

The historical ironies of Oak Woods continue in the world of baseball. Player and manager Cap Anson and early baseball commissioner Kenesaw "Mountain" Landis, both baseball pioneers and both of whom fought to keep African-Americans out of baseball, are buried near one of the most progressive men in baseball history, Bill Veeck, who signed Larry Doby, the first African-American player in the American League.

Finally, many of the infamous rest side by side with the famous, including Jake "Greasy Thumbs" Guzic, Jim Collisimo, Leopold Loeb, and the mayor who presided over Chicago during Prohibition in the era of Al Capone and Bugs Moran, William "Big Bill" Thompson.

OAK WOODS CEMETERY IS CLOSE TO AN-other important site for Chicago African-American history, the **Du Sable Museum of African-American History**. Founded by Dr. Margaret Burroughs in 1961, the museum contains one of the nation's largest collections of African-American paintings, drawings, and sculptures. It also contains over 50,000 artifacts along with their newest permanent exhibit, "A Slow Walk to Greatness," honoring former Chicago mayor Harold Washington. The museum is located at 740 East 56th Place (773/947-0600), and is open Monday through Saturday 10:00 AM–5:00 PM and Sundays Noon–5:00 PM. The cemetery is also located near Chicago's oldest restaurant, **Daley's Restaurant** at 809 E. 63rd Street (see p. 81). Finally, no visit to Woodlawn would be complete without a visit to **Jimmy's Woodlawn Tap** (1172 E. 55th St., 773/643-5516), an institution for University of Chicago students, professors, and neighborhood regulars. The bar's menu features burgers, Italian beefs, and Rueben sandwiches, and there is usually an open jazz jam on Saturday nights. The bar accommodates drinkers morning, noon, night, and back into the morning: it's open from 10:30 AM–2:00 AM, Monday through Friday; 11:00 AM–3:00 AM on Saturday; and 11:00 AM–2:00 AM on Sundays.

OLDEST CHURCH BUILDING

OLD SAINT PATRICK'S CHURCH
123 S. Desplaines Street
(1846, parish; 1856, building)

I n 1846, Irish immigrants founded the second Catholic parish in Chicago, and named it after St. Patrick, the Apostle of Ireland. Augustus Bauer and Asher Carter, two of the city's first architects, designed it. The cornerstone for the church was laid on May 22, 1853, and the church was dedicated on Christmas Day, 1856.

From the start, St. Patrick's parish and church thrived. Only a year after it was dedicated, Reverend Denis Dunne brought the St. Vincent De Paul Society to Chicago, helping to fulfill the church's mission of aiding the less fortunate. By good fortune or perhaps holy intervention, the Great Chicago Fire passed just two blocks from the church, making it one of the few structures to survive the massive conflagration. Chicago and the church

continued to grow. In 1885, the spires of the church were designed and completed. A Celtic art exhibit at the Columbian
Exposition of 1893 inspired Thomas O'Shaughnessy to design,
build, and install 15 stained glass windows. Taken from Ireland's
Book of Kells, the stained glass windows include Faith, Hope,
and Charity, also known as the Terence MacSwiney Memorial
Triptych. The final installation was completed in 1922, ending a
30-year project.

As time passed, the neighborhood around the church
changed. The majority of Irish immigrants had long since called
Bridgeport and areas of the North and Northwest Sides their
home. More and more, the area around St. Pat's was occupied
by businesses. On Sundays, loyal parishioners traveled to the
church from all parts of the city. Eventually, their numbers began to diminish. As people moved farther out to the suburbs in
the 1950s, the size of the parish dwindled. The school closed.
Finally, the construction of the Kennedy Expressway led to the
razing of the few remaining homes in the area. St. Patrick's was
stuck between large streets and busy highways and had lost its
appeal. The building was listed on the National Register of Historic Places in 1977, but it did little good. By 1983, the parish had
only four registered members.

Throughout Chicago's history, priests like the Reverend
Arnold Damen and Archbishop James Quigley helped build
churches, schools, and neighborhoods. When he became pastor
of St. Pat's Church in 1983, the Reverend John J. Wall also took
on a formidable challenge. He looked over a church with lan-
guishing membership and waning finances. It was during this
time that he unveiled a plan called "the church for the market-
place." Realizing that the old, blue-collar immigrant tradition
was outdated, he began targeting working professionals. Wall
saw in second or third generation immigrants a need to return
to the roots and social structure that the church provided. He

also saw the church as a gathering place and meeting ground for the new, young, and single residents of the city. In 1985 he organized the first "World's Largest Block Party," an annual outdoor street festival that now draws tens of thousands of people.

By 1987, St. Patrick's Sunday attendance had grown to two thousand people. In 2006, the church celebrated 160 years of faith. Today, it stands as the oldest building in Chicago.

Old St. Pat's is located just west of the Kennedy Expressway at 123 South Desplaines Street. Take a short detour off the expressway and step inside. After all, how many of you have actually been in a Chicago building that is over 150 years old?

THE BUILDING OF THE KENNEDY EXPRESS-way in the 1960s essentially divided the neighborhood around Old St. Patrick's in half, making it much less family friendly. Now the area is occupied by a new generation of younger, urban pioneers, as well as a few large warehouses and offices. A nearby favorite and "oldest," perfect before or after a visit to the church is the veteran breakfast diner **Lou Mitchell's** (see Oldest Breakfast Restaurant, p. 140). The real action around St. Patrick's, however, is **Greektown** (Halsted Street between Monroe Street and Jackson Boulevard), three blocks west. With over 20 Grecian flavored bars, restaurants, and shops, it offers some of the most festive and inexpensive dining in Chicago. (For more on Greektown, see **Athenian Candle**, Oldest Religious Goods Store, p. 129.)

OLDEST FAMILY-OWNED BUSINESS OLDEST TOBACCO SHOP

IWAN RIES & CO.
19 S. Wabash Avenue
(1857)

In recent times, laws and ordinances may have tamped down on cigar and pipe smoking, but after 150 years, Iwan Ries rolls on.

It all started when Chicago was still a rough and tumble, "western" town in the 1850s. In 1857, German immigrant Edward Hoffman arrived in Chicago. While many businesses' survival depends on the economy, the pipe business rides ebbs and flows of popular fashion and culture. When Hoffman arrived, practically every photo of an important man was taken as he smoked a cigar or a pipe. Hoffman decided to sell tobacco.

The company started in Chicago's famous Sherman House hotel. Hoffman immediately concentrated on the market of gentlemen and tourists. During the Great Chicago Fire the

Sherman House burnt to the ground, but the owners quickly rebuilt. In 1898, cigars were at the height of fashion, so Hoffman decided to call for help. "In 1898 my great grandfather's uncle, Edward Hoffman, called on his nephew Iwan Ries to help run the business," Kevin Levi, who represents the fifth generation in the business, says. "While Hoffman became involved with the more lucrative manufacturing, he slowly began to turn the retail business over to his nephew, who changed the name of the company to Iwan Ries and Co."

The invention of rolling machines made cigarettes cheap and accessible. As cigarettes gained popularity with soldiers during World War I, they began to slowly take over the tobacco market. Cigar-smoking gangsters and pipe-smoking gentlemen still helped Ries roar through the 1920s.

Then, he passed the business on. "Ries did not have any sons, so he turned the business over to his daughter Rosalie in 1929," Levi says. "She married my grandfather, Stanly Levi, who joined the business that year. Even though 1929 was the first year of the Great Depression, the business did well. I guess people wanted to smoke their troubles away."

People kept finding reasons to keep smoking well beyond the Great Depression. "The 1950s and 1960s were the golden age of pipe smokers," Levi says. "You had popular figures like Bing Crosby, James Stewart, and Robert Young, who played the character of Jim Anderson, the father of *Father Knows Best*, all smoking pipes. During the 1960s the professorial look was in. It was the fashion for college students to wear a tweed jacket with the patches on the sleeves and smoke a pipe." It was also around that time that Norman Rockwell depicted the idealized image of the mature, confident, and loving father, reading the paper with the family pet at his feet, smoking a pipe.

The 1990s saw the "cigar boom." Once again it was led by celebrities and popular culture. This time, male alpha figures like Arnold Schwarzenegger, Mike Ditka, and Jack Nicholson encouraged men across the country to light up—cigars were not only classy, they implied that smoking a cigar meant you were tough as well.

Today, the name of Iwan Ries insures a steady stream of smokers looking for fine tobacco to accompany their brandy or whiskey. The store caries over one hundred brands of tobacco and eight hundred different cigars. They also carry over ten thousand different pipes, ranging in price from $20 to $25,000. Walk into the small but comfortable shop—the aromatic mixture of cigar and pipe tobaccos fills the air. Many of these tobaccos are Ries's own Three Star Blends. Pick up some Three Star Dutch, Three Star Ebony, and Three Star Banner Lite—and you'll discover why generations of pipe smokers swear by them.

☞ IN THE OLD DAYS YOU COULD BUY A FINE cigar and pipe at Iwan Reis, then head over to a local establishment and enjoy it along with a good meal. Unfortunately for some, pipe and cigar smoking, as well as puffing on a cigarette, is now downright illegal in all bars, restaurants, and public buildings in Chicago. But generations of big shots have lit up at **Miller's Pub** (134 S. Wabash Ave., 312/263-4988). Miller's is as old Chicago as old Chicago can get. The haunt of celebrities like Harry Caray, Bill Veeck, and Chicago native and Amundsen High School graduate Bob Fosse, the menu is no-nonsense guy food like roast beef sandwiches, steaks, prime rib, and Canadian baby back ribs, with salads, fish, and seafood for the rest of you. An eclectic hodgepodge of stained glass, stuffed deer heads, and oil paintings of Chicago celebrities, it is dark, homey, crowded, and open until 4 AM daily (kitchen closes earlier). It also sports the best collection of celebrity photos in the city, including legends Humphrey Bogart, Babe Ruth, Frank Sinatra, and Tony Bennett, to go along with your usual array of athletes, newscasters, and Jay Leno, who seems to have his picture everywhere.

OLDEST SHIPWRECK

THE *LOUISVILLE*
Lake Michigan, east of the
Illinois–Indiana border
(1857)

n a warm summer weekend, a look out towards the waters of Lake Michigan will yield an eyeful of puffy white sails, and pleasure yachts moored near the beaches. However, during the 1800s, Chicago's lakefront and the downtown riverfront more resembled Hong Kong Harbor. Schooners, clippers, barges, and steamships could be viewed offshore for as far as the eye could see. The Chicago River and its inland harbors held an even greater assortment of floating vessels. Sailing dinghies, oar boats, rowboats, tugboats, as well as homemade fishing boats and crude barges fashioned from wooden planks and barrels turned the riverfront into a giant freshwater maze.

Like today's expressways, the traffic created more than its share of fatal accidents. The most famous of these is the *Lady Elgin*. Often referred to as "the Titanic of the Great Lakes," it went down off the coast of Waukegan at the cost of over three hundred lives. The oldest shipwreck, however, is the *Louisville*. A 140-foot steamer that weighed over 366 tons, it sank on September 29, 1857. Just like the boat accidents on the Mississippi, the high-pressure boilers' steam engine exploded. The resulting destruction left little visible wreckage. Diver Rick Drew described it as "a tangle of pipes, partial stack, and a huge pile of anchor chain." It is located off the shores of Northwest Indiana, approximately six miles east of Chicago. Other old-time wrecks include the *Wings of the Wind*, a 130-foot schooner that sank in 1866 some three and one-half miles off the Wilson Avenue crib, and the David Dows, a five-masted schooner that sank near the *Louisville* in 1889.

LOCATED NOT FAR FROM THE SUNKEN REmains of the *Louisville* is the **Wilson Avenue "crib"** (41 50/58 degrees north by 87 35/28 degrees west), a large building located off of Lake Michigan that gathers water for drinking and other uses. The Wilson Avenue crib utilizes a series of pumps, which takes fresh, cold water from tunnels 200 feet below the surface and brings it up with pipes that are 10–20 feet in diameter.

A round, brick and cement building resembling an ancient fortress, the crib used to be staffed by four crib tenders whose job it was to check the pumps and gauges, make minor repairs, and dynamite ice in the winter. They also got a hell of a view of the lake and city skyline. Now the machines are mostly automated, but the crib remains a beacon for boats and a curiosity for those gazing across the waters from the lakeshore.

JAEGER FUNERAL HOME
3526 N. Cicero Avenue
(1858)

B y the end of the nineteenth century, Chicago was home to tens of thousands of Irish, Italian, Jewish, Polish, and Scandinavian immigrants. The first major wave of Europeans to come to Chicago, however, were German; by 1850 at least 15 percent of Chicago's population consisted of German-born immigrants. Around that time, Joseph Jaeger, the first of five generations at Jaeger Funeral Home, moved to Chicago.

While many Germans from rural backgrounds settled on farms throughout the Midwest, the skilled tradesmen and artisans quickly found work in American cities. Joseph Jaeger fell into this category. "My great, great grandfather was a cabinet maker and coffin maker from Germany who helped to build the first German conciliate here," Douglas Jaeger, director of the Jaeger Funeral Home says. "Their original location was on Canal, near Lake Street." As the first major business district in Chicago, the Canal and Lake Street area was the home to many pioneer establishments, including the original Peacock Jewelers. While most of the larger businesses moved southeast to the Wabash and Randolph area during the 1850s, the Jaeger Funeral Home remained.

That is, it remained until the Great Chicago Fire destroyed it in 1871. The tragedy of the fire prompted Joseph Jaeger to pass the business on to his sons, Adam and Otto, who moved the business to 12th Street and Halsted Street, where it stayed until 1895. That year, Adam and Otto moved the business to 2313–2315 West North Avenue, in the midst of a large community of German immigrants. It was during this time that the business flourished. Jaeger explains, "The business took up almost half a block, as we had a stable and many horse-drawn carriages. The person responsible for this was my great grandfather Otto. He was six-foot-eight, three hundred pounds, so he quickly became a well-recognized figure in the community." Jaeger Funeral Home stayed in that German stronghold until the 1960s. Then the business moved again, this time to 3526 North Cicero Avenue.

Douglas Jaeger represents the fifth generation of Jaegers working in the second oldest family-run business in the city. "I went to Northeastern and worked in the printing business for a while, but I came back to work in the family business a short time later," Jaeger says. "For me, it was almost like a calling."

Even though the German community is scattered throughout the city and suburbs, the Jaegers still keep a loyal clientele. "A lot of people from the neighborhood have moved to the suburbs, but we still have a long-term rapport with their families," Jaeger says. "So what they often do is call me, and I will make all the funeral arrangements. But since they live in the suburbs, we hold the actual service at a funeral home outside of the city, closer to their homes. We have our staff there and collect a fee, but I arrange to just use a different space for the actual service. People are doing this more and more, which is very flattering to me, and says something about our tradition and five generations of service in the community."

LOCATED ON THE OUTSKIRTS OF THE PORtage Park neighborhood, the Jaeger Funeral Home is near one of the Northwest Side's theatrical treasures, the **Portage Theater** (4050 N. Milwaukee Ave., 773/736-4050). Built in 1920, the Portage could have been the oldest movie theater, but the Portage no longer regularly shows movies. Instead, it is a kind of cultural oasis for the area, a place to host independent and student films, film festivals, ethnic films, ethnic music presentations, fan events, holiday sing-alongs, and other curiosities, including once an appearance by Ricky Lee Jones. One of the most notable of these is the annual celebration of silent film produced by **The Silent Film Society of Chicago** (www.silentfilmchicago.com, 773/205-SFSC). Fridays in July and August are a time when the likes of Chaplin, Keaton, and Fairbanks once again light up the silver screen, often accompanied by a live organ or even a small orchestra. Dennis Wolkowicz, a resident of the Northwest Side and former president of the Silent Film Society, has been largely responsible for returning the Portage to its original splendor and rightful cultural role.

OLD CHICAGO WATER TOWER
Michigan Avenue at Chicago Avenue
(1859)

I t is one of the most recognizable landmarks in Chicago. The symbol of the Magnificent Mile and the City that Works, the Water Tower has appeared on thousands of promotional and tourist photographs and its likeness broadcast over national television, and in films and videos. Unlike many icons that garner attention, the story behind the Old Chicago Water Tower is as good as any myth.

The Water Tower was built in 1869 as a standpipe to balance out the pressure created by the pumping station across the street. This structure represented one of the first major steps city leaders took to bring clean water from Lake Michigan into homes throughout Chicago's budding downtown area. It was their hope to put an end to the cholera epidemics that had wiped out substantial portions of Chicago's early population. But the Old Water Tower gained fame and immortality because of another Chicago tragedy, the Chicago Fire of 1871. Some of the most astounding photos ever taken in Chicago feature men pushing wheel barrows of rubble amidst the blocks and blocks of charred ruins created by the fire.

W. W. Boyington, a renowned architect of early Chicago, designed the building. Fittingly, it is made of limestone from Joliet, Illinois, a material that was to become the basis for many of Chicago's great early buildings. A crude, pioneer imitation of Gothic style, the water tower is fitted with dozens of mini-towers, arched windows and doors, pinnacles, and cupolas. The top spire, which reaches 156 feet, is surrounded by more narrow windows and arches. The inside was constructed of 168 columns, all corniced by solid oak beams 12 inches in diameter. Artistically, the Old Water Tower is a mash-up of a Gothic church, Irish castle, and medieval fortress. Upon visiting Chicago in 1882, Oscar Wilde remarked that the building was "a castellated monstrosity with pepperboxes stuck all over it."

The building was rebuilt from 1913 through 1916. During this span, every piece of limestone was replaced, mostly by volunteers with a can-do spirit that demonstrated Chicago's growing position as a world-class city. In 1969, the American Water Works Association named the building America's First Water Landmark. On October 6, 1971, one hundred years after the Great Chicago Fire, the building was designated a Chicago landmark.

In the following years, the Old Water Tower and its sister building across the street, the Old Chicago Pumping Station, were converted into tourist information centers and galleries containing the art and photographs of famous and aspiring Chicago artists. The Lookingglass Theatre now uses the Pumping Station as its headquarters.

Chicago's Water Tower has also gained notoriety through rumors of ghosts haunting the old structure. "Since the rebuilding of the Near North Side, passersby have frequently glimpsed the apparition of a man hanging in one of the windows of the Chicago Water Tower," writes *Chicago Haunts* author Ursula Bielski. "Paranormal researchers in Chicago are uncertain about the origin of the apparition, but it's likely that the phenomenon stems from the days after the Fire itself, when Chicagoans lived under martial law. In the wake of the Fire, looting and further burning became the order of the day, inspiring a curfew and a decree that anyone who did not answer to police should be shot—or hanged—immediately."

It is certain that millions of visitors—living or otherwise—still frequent the Old Water Tower. For as long as it stands, it will remain one of the most recognizable symbols of not only the Magnificent Mile, but the city of Chicago as well.

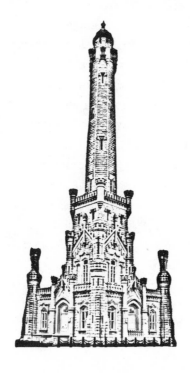

👉 ACROSS THE STREET AND A BIT TO THE north of the old Water Tower is **Water Tower Place** (835 N. Michigan Ave.), one of the best known shopping centers in the Midwest, complete with eateries and every kind of luxury store you can imagine. But if you are looking for something more in the "oldest" line, the **Allerton Hotel** (701 N. Michigan Ave., 312/440-1500) adds quite a bit more to the city's historic tapestry. A 25-story hotel, the Allerton is known for its pronounced shape—containing four towers and a set-back middle portion, light brownstone exterior, and 20-foot-high white letters that read, *Allerton Hotel Tip Top Tap*. During its heyday, it was the kind of place where uniformed bellhops, wearing pillbox hats, took guests' bags and directed them to the Tip Top Tap for refreshment, an establishment rivaling San Francisco's Top of the Mark for its combination of elegance and downtown view. The Tip Top Tap is where the "Moscow Mule," a drink made of vodka, ginger beer, lime, and bitters, became popular. During the morning hours, the room was host to *Don McNeil's Breakfast Club*, a nostalgic favorite for radio fans. During the 1980s, disc jockey Steve Dahl hosted *The Coho Breakfast Club*, a tribute to the radio pioneer, in the same hotel. In the mid-60s, the hotel began to decline and the Tip Top Tap closed for good. In 1998, the building was declared a Chicago Landmark, setting it on the path to a $60 million renovation in 1999, proof of what landmark status can do. Today, the hotel thrives as a more mature alternative to the newer hotels that have sprung up along the Mag Mile. The sign, *Allerton Hotel Tip Top Tap*, still hangs over the top floor, and plenty of visitors still eagerly wander into the building only to learn that the Tip Top Tap is closed.

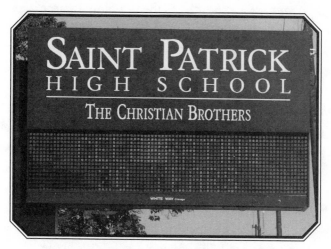

ST. PATRICK HIGH SCHOOL
5900 W. Belmont Avenue (new location)
(1861)

After establishing a church at Desplaines and Adams streets, the members of St. Patrick's parish set their sights on a new goal—educating their children. For this task they called on the Christian Brothers of de LaSalle. Not to be confused with the Christian Brothers founded by Edmund Rice (sometimes called the Irish Christian Brothers), this order was established by St. John the Baptist de LaSalle, in Reims, France, in 1680.

"It has always been the tradition that every parish should have a school, so the parishioners, most of them Irish immigrants, began the original school in 1861," Brother Konrad Diebold, president of St. Patrick High School, says. "They offered classes like shorthand, typing, and note taking, primarily to train students for jobs as clerks in the downtown businesses. Luckily the school survived the Chicago Fire, as both the winds and God were on our side," Diebold continues. "After the fire, the school closed down for four months as the building became a food depository and shelter for fire victims."

As Irish, German, and other Catholic immigrant groups continued to arrive in Chicago, the school's attendance increased throughout the late nineteenth and early twentieth centuries. "There were still a lot of residents in the area, and the school stayed strong through the 1920s and into the 30s," Diebold says.

The westward expansion of downtown saw more and more families moving away from the parish. Then, in the 1950s, suburban flight and construction of the Kennedy Expressway a block away meant that drastic measures had to be taken. "In 1953, the Cardinal moved us to Belmont and Austin. While the new building was being prepared, students took classes at Providence St. Mel in the afternoon so as not to miss out on their studies," Diebold explains.

In 1987, the position of president was created. Diebold has held that post for over 23 years. Dr. Joseph Schmidt and his brother Charles Schmidt, who have formed the core of the school's leadership team, joined him.

The school continues to grow and thrive. It has always been a powerhouse in sports (Ray Meyer and several professional athletes are alumni). St. Pat's also added artistic programs and activities, including school publications, an award-winning jazz band, and a theater department whose productions regularly attract not just parents but neighbors from throughout the community. A school of roughly one thousand boys, their productions have included *Over the Tavern*, *Damn Yankees*, *Guys and Dolls*, *Into the Woods*, and *Les Misérables*.

☞ ST. PATRICK HIGH SCHOOL HAS SURVIVED changes in demographics, economics, and educational attitudes across generations and continues to thrive and excel. Unfortunately, the same cannot be said for the **Patio Theatre** (6008 W. Irving Park Rd.). The Patio (often jokingly pronounced the Pay-Show by locals) was given a Spanish Renaissance design by architect Rudolf Wolff and completed in 1927. Like the **Music Box** (see p. 171), it featured a dark ceiling filled with blinking lights, creating the effect of a night time sky. It was the neighborhood movie house for residents of the Irving & Austin/ St. Pascal's area for decades. Showing films well into the 1990s, the Patio was one of the few classic neighborhood movie houses in Chicago not divided into multiple screens. Today, it stands vacant. Neighborhood groups and others have met to preserve the structure but so far no action has been taken.

OLDEST MARKED GRAVE

JOHN KINZIE (DIED IN 1828)
Moved to Graceland Cemetery
4001 N. Clark Street
(late 1860s)

hicago, circa 1869. The death and devastation of the Civil War has ended, and the city's frequent outbreaks of yellow fever and cholera have subsided. Yet there may be few scenes more ghoulish than one that occurred on the Near North Side. Demand for land in what is now Lincoln Park necessitated the relocation of the remains in the Chicago City Cemetery (at Clark Street and North Avenue) and the Roman Catholic Cemetery (at State Street and North Avenue). As a result, almost twenty thousand graves, stretching from Armitage Avenue to North Avenue, were exhumed. Day after day coffins were unearthed, sometimes laying for days in the hot sun and rain, waiting to be transferred. Other times, bones and skulls, which had sunken into the ground through rotted or poorly constructed coffins, were exposed to the elements. The remains were finally transported in flatbed wagons for the three-mile journey from North Avenue to Graceland Cemetery (at 4001 North Clark Street), to Wunder's Cemetery (at 3963 North Clark Street), and other locations. The gravediggers in their black coats and top hats, driving slowly through the city in an endless stream of coffin-filled wagons, is a scene that even Edgar Allen Poe could probably have not imagined.

One of the first bodies to be moved from the City Cemetery to Graceland was that of John Kinzie. Surely, hundreds of settlers were buried in their backyards, along the river, or in the areas surrounding Fort Dearborn and Streeterville, but Kinzie's is the oldest marked grave. In those days, the area was a swamp. Now it contains some of the most expensive real estate in the world. As much as anyone, John Kinzie is responsible for this development.

John Kinzie's life as a trader, settler, pioneer, and veteran of the War of 1812 reads like a James Fenimore Cooper novel. Kinzie was born in 1763 in Quebec City, Canada. When he was 22, he rescued two sisters that had been kidnapped by Shawnee Indians in 1785. In an act of endearing gratitude, one of the young women, Margaret McKinzie, married him. They came to Chicago in 1800 and bought a house at Wolf Point from Jean Baptiste Pointe du Sable. His daughter, Ellen Marion Kinzie, was born in 1804. She is alleged to be the first Caucasian born in Chicago. Kinzie socialized with many local Native Americans and soldiers at Fort Dearborn. As the War of 1812 began, some members of the Potawatomi, Miami, and Winnebago tribes allied with the British, attacked the settlers at the fort, killing not only soldiers, but also women and children. Legend has it that Kinzie was spared by a future Native American chief who "brushed" his hair with an axe, and then violently threw him into the bottom of his canoe. The Indians on shore believed that

he had scalped the white man, and Kinzie was able to escape to
Michigan. Kinzie returned after the war to become an important trader, businessman, and landowner. He died in 1828 and
was buried near his home at Wolf Point. His body was moved
to the City Cemetery a few years later, and, in 1868, transferred
to Graceland.

Graceland Cemetery also contains the memorials of dozens
of famous and influential Chicagoans. The list of people buried
there reads like a Who's Who of the city's founders, architects,
and businessmen. They include George Pullman, Louis Sullivan, Potter Palmer, William Kimball, Daniel Burnham, Joseph
Medill, Allan Pinkerton, Cyrus McCormick, Philip Armour,
Ludwig Mies van der Rohe, Marshall Field, Richard Nickel,
Charles Wacker, Peter Schoenhofen, and William Goodman.
Former heavyweight champion boxer Jack Johnson is also interred in Graceland.

For many, a trip to a cemetery might seem morbid, but mus-
ter your wild side and take a walk inside Graceland Cemetery,
especially in the morning hours or at dusk. The architecture
and design of the grave markers, the quiet tranquility, and the
sense of history may inspire thoughts and visions far beyond
the scope of your television remote. Then, if you want a food
or alcohol fix, the bars and restaurants of Wrigleyville begin just
two blocks to the south.

Other old and interesting graves in Chicago include The
Couch Tomb (Ira Couch,1806–1857), which still stands on the
grounds of the old City Cemetery across from the Chicago History Museum. There is also the grave of Boston Tea Party survi-
vor David Kennison (1736–1852). Located across from the farm
in Lincoln Park Zoo, the grave is represented by a small marker
located near what was once a horseshoe pit. Technically, both
the Couch and Kennison gravesites are older than the Kinzie
gravesite. The Kinzie grave was chosen for overall longevity.

Che-Che Pin-Quay (Alexander Robinson), a local Indian chief and the last surviving Native American chief in Chicago, along with members of his family, are buried in Robinson Woods at Lawrence Avenue and East River Road.

ODDLY ENOUGH, GRACELAND IS FOUR blocks north on Clark Street from **Wrigley Field** (see Oldest Ballpark, p. 123) and **Wrigleyville**, one of the liveliest neighborhoods in town. Just steps from the final resting place of the famous are wall-to-wall bars, nightclubs, and restaurants, including **The Metro** (3730 N. Clark St., 773/549-0203), Chicago's oldest and best known rock club. Seven blocks due west of the cemetery is the **Orange Garden Restaurant** (see Oldest Chinese Restaurant and Oldest Neon Sign, p. 147).

OLDEST SCHOOL BUILDING

ST. IGNATIUS COLLEGE PREP
1076 W. Roosevelt Road
(1869)

While St. Patrick's is the oldest school in Chicago, St. Ignatius College Prep is the oldest school building.

In the mid-1800s, many Europeans still considered Chicago a cholera-filled, backwoods swamp. The Jesuits deemed it necessary to send a missionary. Reverend Arnold Damen (for whom Damen Avenue is named) arrived in Chicago from Holland in 1857. Father Damen built a parish on the prairie at the city limits. Within one year, the church became a haven for the Irish immigrants who were flocking to the area. "St. Ignatius always served the immigrant community," John Chandler, vice-president of the school, says. "At first it was the German and Irish, then the Italian, Greek, and Jewish—St. Ignatius began admitting Jewish students in the late nineteenth century—and later the African-Americans who migrated here after both world wars, and now the Hispanics. The school has always been a rich tapestry."

The school was structured after the European model of three years of high school (St. Ignatius Prep) and three years of college. Classes began in 1870. In 1871, luck and what many call "holy intervention" saved the school from destruction after its first anniversary. "The Great Chicago Fire started in the area of the O'Leary house, which was just five blocks west of here," Chandler says. "It was heading this way when the wind suddenly shifted and spared the building. It is part of St. Ignatius lore that Father Damen was in Brooklyn. When he heard about the fire he spent the night in a vigil so that the church and school would be saved. When it was, he promised to keep a vigil of seven candles burning in front of the picture of Our Lady of Perpetual Help. To this day, candles are still burning there."

The school expanded through the early part of the next century. Attendance grew so high that Archbishop Quigley gave permission for the Jesuits to establish a college on another "new frontier," the North Side of Chicago. In 1906, the school purchased land near Lake Michigan, Sheridan Road, and the Chicago, Milwaukee, St. Paul and Pacific Railroad (now the tracks are part of the CTA Red Line). Between 1906 and 1924, St. Ignatius spent roughly $400,000 to set up Loyola University, and in 1924 the two entities officially separated.

In the years following World War II, the trend in enrollment reversed. Much of the community fled to the suburbs as the construction of University of Illinois at Chicago and the Eisenhower Expressway tore up their old Italian, Greek, and Jewish neighborhods. Many Catholic schools followed. A fire in 1953 caused $160,000 in damage to St. Ignatius and forced the issue even further. According to Chandler, "during the 1950s, the school seriously considered moving to the suburbs, but many felt that by moving we would be abandoning the very people who helped establish our school, and that the school—and the Jesuits—should always have a presence in the central city."

St. Ignatius not only remained, but it began a slow, steady renovation. Walking through the school today is like walking through a museum. The floors are covered with thick, sculptured carpeting. Plaster statues and bronze busts, baby grand pianos, chandeliers, and fireplaces give the place an atmosphere of an old English boarding school. The ceiling of the library is over three stories high and contains a massive fresco relief. It features portraits of important Chicago historical figures such as Carl Sandburg, Jane Addams, and Ida B. Wells, painted in gold and framed by laurels, in a style reminiscent of Roman coins. Painted or etched on the walls are sayings by prominent people, including artist Pablo Picasso's "Computers are useless for they only give you answers." The area that used to be the science room is made of hand-carved butternut wood. The school's cafeteria features granite walls, and portions of the hardwood flooring are sculpted in an ornate pattern inspired by St Mark's Cathedral.

To add to this historic and architectural ambiance, the school has obtained plaster reliefs, terra cotta ornamentation, chairs, statues, and whole sections of walls from some of the most architecturally significant buildings in the city. "Over the years we were able to salvage the panels from the outer walls of the Chicago Stadium (which are now the outside of our physical education complex), portions of the Civic Opera House, part of the facade that Louis Sullivan designed for the Chicago Stock Exchange, and ornamental works from the Civic Theatre in the Opera House, the Auditorium Theatre, Garrick Theater, Granada Theater, State–Lake Theater, Roosevelt Theater, and Paradise Theater," Chandler says.

The school also features many interior gardens. Placed among the flowers, scrubs, and tall pine trees are the ten-foot statue of the town crier taken from the former offices of the *Chicago Herald* newspaper and a sculpture of Diana the Huntress. Used as the pinnacle of the tower for Stanford White's original Madison Square Garden, it is one of the most recognizable statues of its kind in the nation.

In 1979 St. Ignatius College Prep began to admit girls, and throughout the next half-century it experienced an increase in enrollment. The school was awarded the National Trust for Historic Preservation Honor Award in 1988. In 1995, 1,278 students, the largest group ever, graduated from the school. The school remains a beautiful, active, and enduring monument to Chicago's pursuit of education.

JUST SOUTH OF ST. IGNATIUS IS ANOTHER relic from Chicago's earliest days. The **Engine Company 18 Firehouse** (1123 W. Roosevelt Rd.) dates back to 1873. Made from cut stone, it featured all brass rails, bells, and other paraphernalia. The building still has a hole in the roof where hay was once shoveled down from the station's hay loft, as well an area that used to house horses. The station was in use until August 2, 2008, making it then, the oldest firehouse. But on that date, Mayor Daley dedicated a new ultra-modern firehouse for the neighborhood at 1360 South Blue Island Avenue. Featuring state of the art radio and communications equipment, truck and parts bays, and a modern kitchen and living area, as well as solar panels, water retention devices, and other green technologies, the new firehouse offers a sleeker, safer base for protecting both citizens and firefighters. Proposals for the old firehouse include turning it into a Chicago Fire Department and Safety Workers Museum.

OLDEST HOTEL

 PALMER HOUSE
17 E. Monroe Street
(1871)

A long with names like Joseph Sears, Oscar Mayer, and Gus Swift, Potter Palmer is one of Chicago's early tycoons whose name survives through his business. Originally a native of New York, Palmer began his retail career in Chicago when he opened a dry goods store on Lake Street in 1852. Never one to shun the spotlight, Palmer named his store Potter Palmer and Company. At a time when Chicago was seen as a swamp or rural outpost by many (it had only been incorporated as a city for 14 years), Palmer's business flourished by selling high-end clothing, housewares, and food items to female customers. In 1865, he sold his business to Marshall Field. Incorporating many of Palmer's practices, such as selling upscale merchandise and employing a "no questions asked" return policy, Field became one of the world's most famous merchants.

Palmer sunk his profits from the store into real estate, buying a stretch of State Street between (roughly) Jackson Boulevard and Lake Street. Today, the land is worth billions of dollars, but Palmer's millions were enough to make him one of the wealthiest men in Chicago.

To show off his newfound wealth, he built his first hotel, then known as "The Palmer." It was completed on September 26, 1871. October 8 was the first day of the Great Chicago Fire. The devastation burned a swath through State Street and reduced 32 buildings, coach houses, stables, and storage sheds to rubble; more devastation would follow. In the days following the fire, Palmer took the lead in encouraging others to rebuild Chicago. Instead of merely acting as a booster, Palmer took out a personal loan for $1.7 million (the largest of its day) and immediately set out to reconstruct the hotel.

Working around the clock, often by torchlight, workers rebuilt the hotel in two years. The second version, known as America's first "fireproof hotel," deserved the many comparisons to the grandest hotels in New York and Europe. Designed by John M. Van Osdel, the hotel featured a "vertical steam railroad"—the first elevator. It was also the first hotel to have electricity. It is said that the floor of the hotel's barbershop was paved with silver dollars.

In the proceeding years dignitaries such as Mary Todd Lincoln, Grover Cleveland, Mark Twain, Ulysses S. Grant, Charles Dickens, Oscar Wilde, and Sarah Bernhardt enjoyed the hotel's amenities. One celebrity who apparently did not enjoy the hotel was author Rudyard Kipling. In a passage provided by the Chicago History Museum, Kipling saw Chicago as a city "full of savages." He described the Palmer House as "a gilded and mirrored rabbit-warren, and there I found a huge hall filled with tessellated marble, crammed with people talking about money and spitting about everywhere. Other barbarians charged in and out of this inferno with letters and telegrams in their hands, and yet others shouted at each other. A man who had drunk quite as much as was good for him told me that this was 'the finest hotel in the finest city on God Almighty's earth.'"

The stock market boom of the 1920s drew an even greater need for a luxury hotel. So the Palmer House was rebuilt in stages between 1924 and 1929. By that time, the hotel had been passed to Palmer's sons Honoré (Bertha's maiden name) and Potter Palmer II.

The new Palmer House featured two sections and a lobby. Besides golden angels that adorned barrel-vaulted ceilings worthy of a European palace, the hotel featured candelabras made by Tiffany and 14-carat gold leaf framed murals and artwork restored by Lido Lippi, the same man who restored the Sistine Chapel. The Palmer House was also home of the Empire Room, a luxurious ballroom touted to be the most elegant in Chicago. A team of world-renowned chefs prepared the gourmet food. While dining, guests were entertained over the years by the likes of Louis Armstrong, Benny Goodman, Barbra Streisand, and Sonny and Cher. The lobby became a favorite meeting spot for local dignitaries and politicians, and it hosted victory celebrations for both Richard J. and Richard M. Daley and rallies for President Bill Clinton during the 1996 Democratic National Convention.

As part of the fourth renovation, completed in 2009, the Palmer House restored its one thousand guest rooms. A new 4,000-square-foot penthouse and 3,500-square-foot manager's apartment were added. Potter Palmer and his wife Bertha, known for their lavish parties at their Lake Shore Drive mansion, would be proud.

☞ THE PALMER HOUSE IS FILLED WITH BARS, restaurants, and other diversions. Sweetly situated in the heart of Chicago's Loop, it is surrounded by more of the same. From there it's a short walk to both Millennium and Grant parks. Although **Millennium Park** (Michigan Ave., between Randolph St. and Monroe St.) boasts spitting fountains and "The Bean," **Grant Park** (between Michigan Ave. & Lake Shore Dr. and Randolph St. & the Museum Campus near Roosevelt Rd.) has held Chicago's greatest outdoor treasure, **Buckingham Fountain** (Columbus Dr. & Columbus Pkwy.), since 1927. Operating between mid-April and mid-October, it pumps 14,000 of its 1.5 million gallons of water per minute. At night, it is a kaleidoscope of colors, with reds, greens, blues, and oranges shooting into the air.

OLDEST STABLE

 NOBLE HORSE
1410 N. Orleans Street
(1872)

Most of the reminders of Chicago's past have been torn down, dragged away, and lost for good. Some still remain, usually in the form of old buildings, signs, or statues. But on a cool summer morning at the corner of Sedgwick and Schiller there is one living sign of days long gone. A dozen horses, tails brushing off the occasional fly, meander through an open field, grazing on grass and hay. They are all residents of the Noble Horse.

The stable survived the Great Chicago Fire, the advent of the horse-drawn carriage, economic downturns and depressions, changes in social custom, and, most recently, a plethora of local politicians and developers drooling over what is now prime real estate. "The permits for the building were issued in 1871 and the original structure was built in 1872. Most of it was torched during the Great Chicago Fire, but it was rebuilt only a few months later," shares Dan Sampson, owner of Noble Horse and Noble Horse Equestrian Theater.

When Noble Horse was first built, draft horses delivered almost everything in the city and people got around town by carriage or saddled mare. When cars, trucks, and buses began to overtake Chicago's streets, Noble Horse was overhauled, the first of many incarnations. "A man named Tim Samuelson, a leading Chicago historian and preservationist from the Chicago Historical Society, did a lot of research on this place and said that in 1922 there was a big renovation, more than likely involved with the Marshall Field Town and Gardens, a local housing development," Sampson says.

Noble Horse survived through the urban renewal of the 1950s and the Hippie boom of the 1960s. "It was used as a private stable for residents of Lincoln Park and other city neighborhoods who owned horses," Sampson says. "They would ride down Schiller to Dearborn and across into Lincoln Park. There was also an indoor circuit known as the Indian Riding Area, where people trained horses and took lessons to practice for equestrian events." In 1979, Mayor Jane Byrne decided that carriage rides would add class and charm to Chicago's Loop. In 1985, Noble Horse became the official stable for the downtown carriages. It was about this time that Sampson became involved in the business.

"My father was a rider and a breeder, my grandfather was a breeder and farmer as well, so you can definitely say that horses are in my blood," Sampson says. He spent his childhood learning to ride and choreograph show horses on an expansive family farm. He was fortunate to be a member of the United States Marine Corps from 1971 to 1976. "There weren't a lot of people who knew too much about horses in the Marines at that time, so they called on me to develop a mounted unit to perform at the bicentennial," Sampson relates. "I also got to tour Europe, where I learned about the tradition of Cossack riding and the long breeds and bloodlines of horses in Arabia and Spain. Right now we have a Spanish Andalusia, whose bloodlines can be directly traced to 1450."

When Sampson purchased the stables in 1986 the building and arena were run down. He found a partner in 1989 who agreed to finance the rehabilitation of the building, but spent most of the next decade fighting politicians to get the structure rebuilt. Sampson says that the stable was formerly a part of the 42nd Ward, where he had issues with Alderman Burton Natarus and Second Ward Alderman Wallace Davis Jr. "We wanted to rehabilitate the building but had to fight for years to get it rezoned. One day a representative from Alderman Wallace Davis Jr.'s office came in and basically said that it would take $8,000 to fill out and administer the paperwork. I think a few years later he was convicted as part of a bribery scandal involving city aldermen." (Records indicate that Davis was convicted as part of Chicago's Silver Shovel investigation. In 2007 he was one of seven aldermanic candidates to run for office despite a prior conviction, proving that some things never change in Chicago.)

Sampson persisted, and renovations to the stable were completed in 2003. Part of the rebuilding effort included the erection of a large, comfortable seating area, box office, and other amenities to be included as part of the Noble Horse Theater. Besides being the owner of the stables and performing jobs such as bringing in hay, training horses, supervising the stables, and trucking animals to nearby farms, Sampson is an expert horseman who performs regularly in the show.

"I got the idea when I saw Medieval Times in San Francisco, but then they built one in the northern suburbs. That was about the time of *Urban Cowboy* [a 1980 film] or the Western swing dance craze of the early 1990s, so we thought 'Wild West Show,' but Chicago's North Side and the Old Town area aren't really a country and western market." Sampson devised a European riding exhibition filled with ornate period costumes, beautiful horses, and equestrian events reminiscent of Austria's Lipizzaner stallion shows. The venue showcases the grace and beauty of the Lipizzaners, along with Arabian horses, and a Spanish Andalusian. The horses jump, tumble, prance, and dance on cue. To perform these tricks, the horse must be trained well and handled by a talented rider. According to Sampson, though, "Nobody rides horses any more, so it is hard to get skilled riders. There are a few western rodeo guys who can do it, but they want nothing to do with 'the big city' so we had to bring in these performers from Kazakhstan, where they have been riding this way for thousands of years."

Like summer stock theater, Noble Horse is on a tight budget, so everybody pitches in to make the shows work. Riders and performers groom and clean the horses, sell pop and candy, clean costumes, and maintain the arena when they are not performing. Besides shows and carriages rides, Noble Horse provides horses for special events. "In the past we did a lot of movie work," Sampson says. "Our horses and riders have appeared in *Risky Business, Babe, The Untouchables* TV show, and lots of other movies and shows. After all, where else are you going to find horses in Chicago?"

The shows, matinees, and dinner performances at Noble Horse run year round. The stable houses as many as 65 horses (which can be rented for $35 per half hour) and 22 carriages ($70 per hour for up to four passengers).

Noble Horse provides an important link to Chicago's prairie past. It is for this reason that we must support this entity, for it is the only link within the Chicago city limits to a time, era, and a noble animal which played a key role in the development of this city. "People forget that a hundred years ago our society was pretty much dependent on horses for all of our local travel," Sampson reminds. "Now we not only have all sorts of motorized vehicles but computers and gadgets as well. These might be more convenient, but they will never be as beautiful or as graceful as a horse."

THERE IS A REASON WHY OLD TOWN IS called Old Town. Settled in the 1830s, its early residents included Michael Diversey, William Ogden, and William Rand. After the Chicago Fire, the area was rebuilt by men like sausage king Oscar Mayer and William Scholl, a podiatrist better known as "Dr. Scholl." The **Old Town Triangle** (bounded by Lincoln Ave., Wells St., and North Ave.) was designated as a Chicago Landmark District in 1977. Combining the ornate wooden homes of San Francisco, the cobblestone courtyards and hidden gardens of New Orleans, and the history of Chicago, Old Town may be the most picturesque area in the city. Among the area's most distinguished homes, though it goes largely unnoticed, is that of **Henry Gerber** (1710 N. Crilly Ct.). Gerber founded the Society for Human Rights, the first chartered organization for gay rights in the United States (1924). Don't miss **St. Michael's Church** (1633 N. Cleveland Ave., 312/642-2498), one of seven buildings to survive the Chicago Fire and the second oldest surviving church in the city (1869), or the **courtyard buildings designed by Louis Sullivan** (1826–34 N. Lincoln Park West). And, if you want a restaurant with the old, Old Town vibe, try **Twin Anchors Restaurant** (1655 N. Sedgwick St., 312/266-1616) famous for its enduring corner-tavern ribs and famous clientele.

OLDEST FUNERAL HOME— SOUTH SIDE

MCINERNEY FUNERAL HOME
4635 S. Wallace Street
(1873)

ucked away on the near Southeast Side, the simple green sign and monogrammed awning are barely noticeable, but the McInerney Funeral Home has been a part of the Chicago landscape for three generations. "My great grandfather started the business with his brothers at 43rd and Union in 1873," Tom Munley, who is carrying on the family tradition, says. "It was run by him and his two brothers, and when the last brother died, he had no direct male heirs, so the business fell to my mom and her three sisters. My mom and aunt had families, and they took over the business in 1952."

In 1893, the owners moved McInerney Funeral Home to its present location at 4635 South Wallace Street (three blocks south and one block east of the original location) in the Canaryville neighborhood. Many legends swirl about as to how the neighborhood got its moniker. One version claims the neighborhood was named after the flocks of sparrows that populated it. Other versions assert that the odor from the nearby stockyards was so strong that homesteaders would place a canary cage on their plot of land. When they returned after a week, a healthy canary meant that the parcel was suitable to live on. The Irish immigrants who moved into the community were a stone's throw from the slaughterhouses, explaining why parts of the area are also called "Back of the Yards."

"When we moved here it was located two blocks from the Chicago Stockyards," Munley relates. "It was so close that we practically had cows running by our front window." At that time, the stockyards were almost a city unto themselves, employing forty thousand people and processing nine million animals a year. The end of the stockyards, however, is just one of the changes McInerney Funeral Home has seen in the last 140 years. "The last stables for the horse-drawn carriages and hearses were torn down and turned into chapels in 1938," Munley says. "When the business first opened, it was common practice for many to have wakes and visitations at the home, but the last home wake here was in 1950. We were also the first funeral home to have air conditioning."

The neighborhood, however, has actually changed very little in the last hundred-plus years. Munley, who began working at the family business in 1975, sees this as the key reason for the longevity of the funeral home. "This has always been a stable neighborhood of basically hard-working people whose lives revolved around St. Gabriel's parish," Munley says. "In recent years we have seen some changes in adjacent Bridgeport, but so far they haven't happened here."

☞ MOST OF THE PHYSICAL EVIDENCE OF CHIcago's Union Stock Yards' storied existence was torn down, hauled away, burned, or eaten when the stockyards closed in 1971. One remaining link is the **Union Stock Yards Arch** (about 100 yards west of Halsted St., between Pershing Rd. and 43rd St.) in the Fuller Park neighborhood. Designed by Burnham and Root in 1875, thousands of stockyard workers filed past the arch on their way to work for almost one hundred years. Today, the white limestone monument is crowned by the relief of "Sherman," a prize-winning bull named after the Civil War general.

 LAKE VIEW HIGH SCHOOL
4018 N. Ashland Avenue
(1874)

brick schoolhouse surrounded by simple wooden homes, livestock pens, stables, open land, and even a graveyard: this was the modest beginning of what is now one of Chicago's most cosmopolitan high schools, Lake View High School.

Nowadays, an advanced degree is often needed for an entry-level professional job, but in the late nineteenth century, a grade school diploma was all that was expected out of most Chicagoans. High school was "higher education," often reserved for families of greater economic means. "The school began in 1874, in what was then called Lake View Township. At that time, this area was not part of Chicago. There was no Chicago public school system. There wasn't even a public high school," Karen

Siciliano, school treasurer, historian, and class of '61 graduate, explains. "Back in those days most people did not go to high school, and college was only for the very well educated. After eighth grade most people went to work."

Lake View High School opened on the corner of Graceland Avenue (now Irving Park Road) and Ashland Avenue with only one teacher and the principal, Dr. Nightingale. He taught eight students. "The first graduate of the school was a boy named Benjamin Franklin McConnell, who graduated in 1876," Siciliano says.

The original building burned to the ground on Friday, May 13, 1885. But it didn't deter Dr. Nightingale. He and the community rebuilt the school in 1886. Over the next five years, the school expanded. "The school originally got its land from Graceland Cemetery, which was one of its first and best-known neighbors," Siciliano says. "In 1889 the township of Lake View was incorporated into the city of Chicago, and the school became part of the Chicago school system." An addition with a gym and assembly hall was built in 1898. In 1939, the school constructed another addition, this one at the far north end of the school on Ashland Avenue.

The baby boom after World War II brought more and more students into the neighborhood. It also coincided with the beginning of a new media era, and Lake View High School was at the forefront. "In 1946 Lake View High School became the first high school to have a TV set, and the first high school TV show was produced at the Lake View TV Center." *Happy Days* star Tom Bosley and famous ventriloquist Edgar Bergen both graduated from Lake View High School. Lake View's diverse, urban look was also one of the settings for the film *My Bodyguard*.

In the 1970s, the Lake View student body grew into a mix of Hispanic, White, Asian, and African-American students. Today, the school still represents the diversity of the city and the surrounding Lakeview neighborhood. Next time you pass through the intersection of Irving Park Road and Ashland Avenue, look past the restaurants, bars, and even the giant Popeye's Chicken franchise across the street. Gaze at the old building in the center of the complex and imagine a time when the area was filled with nothing but tall grass. What is now Lake View High School was a once a little schoolhouse on a prairie.

IN THE HEART OF THE LAKEVIEW NEIGHborhood (now often referred to as "Ravenswood"), Lake View High School is about four blocks west (straight down Irving Park Road) of **Graceland Cemetery** (see p. 42), and about four blocks east of **Orange Garden Restaurant** (see p. 147). Another longtime neighborhood icon is the 24-hour **Diner Grill** (1635 W. Irving Park Rd., 773/248-2030), a cross between Edward Hopper's *Nighthawks at the Diner*, and a set for an off-beat, low-budget, truck-driving horror film starring a ranting, crazed, pre-baby-boomer-mutual funds-spokesperson Dennis Hopper. Its signature offering is The Slinger, a dish that tops a bed of hash browns and grilled onions with two well-done cheeseburgers, two fried eggs, and if you want, ketchup or hot sauce. The crowd varies. In the daytime it's truck drivers and true blue-collar residents. On weekend mornings (2 AM–5 AM) it is a haven for the drunk, stomach-growling, can't-find-anyone-of-the-opposite-sex-so-I-might-as-well-eat crowd.

OLDEST DRUGSTORE

 MERZ APOTHECARY
4716 N. Lincoln Avenue
(1875)

Merz Apothecary predates the widespread use of chemically manufactured drugs, harkening back to a time when medicine meant a combination of teas, herbs, and plants. Instead of Rockwellesque images of pharmacists filling prescriptions while a freckle-faced boy sits at a soda fountain, think *Romeo and Juliet*'s Friar Lawrence blending flowers and herbs for Juliet's forty-hour sleep. With its shelves of jars filled with items like speedwell, stinging nettle, and Swedish bitters, Merz Apothecary sells products that you will never find at Walgreens or CVS.

In 1875, Peter Merz opened a pharmacy near Lincoln and Diversey in a neighborhood of newly arrived German immigrants. The science of modern pharmaceuticals was just beginning.

While many breakthrough drugs like aspirin were being sold, it was also the era of the elixir. Magazine ads and white-suited barkers claimed that one dose of their elixir could cure everything from acne to arthritis, even though the potion was often just a mixture of alcohol and water. Instead of selling chemicals or elixirs, Swiss-born Merz wanted to bring back the tradition of herbal medicines and establish a gathering place for the new European immigrants. "To Merz, it was what a pharmacy used to be back in Switzerland," Anthony Qaiyum, son of the current owner Abdul Qaiyum, says. "He didn't want to split off the link between the natural herbs and remedies and the chemical products. This makes sense because to this day a lot of our mass-produced, prescription drugs are still based on products that come from plants and other natural sources."

Merz Apothecary still thrives after four generations of ownership. Peter passed the business onto his son Lee after World War I, and later Lee passed it down to his sons Melvin, Earl, and Ralph. Together, they survived the fall of the corner drugstore and the rise of the pharmacy chain. But in 1972, Ralph Merz was about to retire without a successor. The store was ready to close when pharmacist Abdul Qaiyum walked in after hearing about it from his German in-laws. After buying the apothecary, he expanded the line of natural products to include skin care, cosmetics, and other health and wellness items. This tied in with the back-to-nature movement of the early 1970s.

Merz gained new customers, but their main customer base started to move out of the area. "I grew up in and around the store," Qaiyum says. "When I was a kid the neighborhood was more German, with places like the Lincoln Turner Hall, Schmelling's Bakery, and Zum Deutschen Eck. A lot of the German and European businesses were moving to Lincoln Square, so in 1982 we moved here." Merz Apothecary now sits on the site of the old Leland Theater, nestled amidst reliable German standbys like the Chicago Brauhaus, transplants like the Old Town School of Folk Music, and newcomers like the Book Cellar. Tin ceilings, hardwood floors, and stained glass windows beautifully decorate the interior.

People come from all over Chicago and the Midwest to shop at Merz Apothecary for remedies such as linden for ailments of the kidney and gall bladder, valerian tea for the nerves, and stinging nettle for arthritis. The apothecary's growing mail-order business at Smallflower.com also delivers these products throughout the nation and the world. "There was a certain period when pharmacies stopped selling these types of natural remedies like teas and herbs because people did not think they were 'modern' but we did not make the split between the natural and chemical." Qaiyum says. "Yes, we are a full-fledged pharmacy with licensed pharmacists who can fill any prescription. But if you want a bottle of Tylenol or a tube of Crest, we figure you can go to any of the hundreds of other places for that."

Luckily, fans of Merz Apothecary won't have to start shopping at chain pharmacies any time soon. "We are in a great area, as Lincoln Square is a melting pot of old European and new, younger people who are interested in our products. That, along with our Internet business, should keep us going for years to come."

FOR DECADES, LINCOLN SQUARE WAS THE focal point of Chicago's German-American community. The **Chicago Brauhouse** (4732 N. Lincoln Ave., 773/784-4444) upholds the tradition of bratwurst, schnitzels, sauerkraut, beer in large steins, and music by men in *liederhosen*. However, restaurants like **Barba Yianni Grecian Taverna** (4761 N. Lincoln Ave., 773/878-6400), which serves the same food as Greektown at even more reasonable prices, the Balkan **Café Bourbon** (4768 N. Lincoln Ave., 773/769-3543), and **La Bocca della Verita** (4618 N. Lincoln Ave., 773/784-6222), an upscale Italian eatery, as well as several quaint coffee shops have turned Lincoln Square into a mini-Europe in Chicago (with lots of hipsters and chic young families to boot). The **Old Town School of Folk Music** (4544 N. Lincoln Ave., 773/728-6000), is the world's largest folk music center, a cultural outpost with a packed schedule of lessons and concerts in just about every musical genre. Around for over 50 years itself, the Old Town School branched out from its Old Town location in 1998 to make the historic Hild Library building its headquarters. Down the street is the **Davis Theater** (4614 N. Lincoln Ave., 773/784-0893), still serving the community after 80 years, thanks to being saved from demolition for condo development by a neighborhood group in 1999. Moving in recent history from a second-run movie theater to art house, it now shows first-run Hollywood films.

OLDEST BAR

SCHALLER'S PUMP
3714 S. Halsted Street
(1881)

here has always been a symbiotic relationship between breweries and taverns. In the days of the old "tied houses," breweries like Schlitz financed Chicago taverns in return for exclusive sales of their product. These practices continue in a different manner today, as the large beer corporations often provide everything from a storefront sign to glasses, coasters, and even free kegs in exchange for (wink, wink) preferential product placement. There is probably no closer relationship in the history of Chicago's breweries and taverns than that between Schaller's Pump and Ambrosia Beer.

In the days before bottles, cans, and even aluminum kegs, beer was delivered in wooden barrels. "Packaged goods" consisted of sending a kid to the neighborhood brewery where he filled a bucket with beer for a nickel. The Ambrosia brewery was located next door to the tavern, and instead of packaging beer into barrels, the brewery piped it directly into Schaller's taps. Thus, Schaller's "Pump," was born.

Schaller's Pump was established on the 3700 block of South Halsted Street, almost butted up against the Chicago stockyards. Perhaps someone like Upton Sinclair's fictional character Jurgis Rudkus in *The Jungle* drank a beer at Schaller's Pump and stood on its sawdust-covered floors. Or maybe Upton Sinclair himself sipped an Ambrosia draft while researching his classic novel.

Unfortunately, the walls of the building can't talk, but Jack Schaller, an octogenarian whose family has run the establishment since the late 1930s, can tell you everything you need to know. "The building has been a bar and restaurant since the late 1880s. Before that, it was a speakeasy. Hey, if you aren't sure, just look at the door," Schaller says. With his daughter Kim looking on, Schaller walks over to the south side of the structure. He points to a heavy wooden door with coats of varnish that are so old and thick they look black. Reaching towards the top, he moves a heavy metal latch to one side. As he moves it, light pours in through a small hole. "During the 1920s this place was a speakeasy," Schaller says. "This was the peek-hole that was used to identify known customers. We kept it the way it was, just for old times' sake."

Known for its slogan, "properly aged and mellowed for particular people," Ambrosia was one of many area breweries. The Manhattan Brewery was located two blocks away at 3901 South Emerald Avenue, and the Canadian Ace Brewery at 3940 South Union Avenue was a stone's throw away. During Prohibition, these breweries were part of Al Capone's, and later Frank Nitti's, empire. There is a very good chance that Nitti and his men made their way through these speakeasy doors. The repeal of Prohibition ended the building's days as a speakeasy and presented the Schaller family with a business opportunity that is still paying dividends today.

"Our family bought the building just after Prohibition," Kim Schaller, who is now the fourth generation of Schallers working at the bar, says. "At that time, Martin Kennelly, one of the first of many mayors from Bridgeport, was mayor." Located across the street from the building that was the 11th Ward Democratic headquarters, Schaller's was a place where precinct captains, city lawyers, and politicians met after plotting the campaigns of Bridgeport natives, including mayors Martin Kennelly, Richard J. Daley, Michael Bilandic, and Richard M. Daley. "My father was the law partner for Richard J. Daley," Schaller says. "But even though he knew about this place, he didn't come in here much. He was more of a quiet, family man."

Gangsters and politicians may have met up at Schaller's Pump over the years, but it has always been a simple, neighborhood hangout. "This has always been an ethnic bar," Jack says. "First we had the Jews along Halsted, and a lot of Lithuanians who came to work at the Stockyards. Then in the 1920s or so the Irish and a few Italians came. Now the neighborhood is predominantly Irish, but there are a lot of Mexicans moving in as well."

Today, with its new developments, bars, restaurants, and a revamped U.S. Cellular Field (formerly Comiskey Park), the Bridgeport neighborhood is attempting to become "Wrigleyville South." Ambrosia Brewery no longer exists, and the spot where it stood is now the parking lot for Schaller's Pump. Still, the bar maintains the neighborhood's historic and ethnic roots. A family business that is also well known for its homemade ribs, pork chops, corned beef and cabbage, butt steaks, and Friday night fish fries, Schaller's hasn't changed much in 125 years. Let's hope it lasts another hundred years, just the way it is.

SCHALLER'S PUMP IS A SYMBOL OF OLD Bridgeport, the Bridgeport of Mayor Richard J. Daley, and a close-knit, blue-collar area. Another vestige from old time BP is the **Ramova Theater** (3518 S. Halsted St.), which, unlike Schaller's, has not been able to endure the area's social and economic changes. Opened in 1929 as a "sister theater" to the Music Box (see Oldest Movie Theater, p. 171), it once had over 1,500 seats and the same faux "starry night" ceiling as the Music Box. The theater was opened to cater to the blue-collar immigrants who lived in the neighborhood. In fact, Ramova means "peaceful place" in Lithuanian. The highlight of the theater's history came in 1940, when, since the subject matter was deemed too controversial for the larger Loop theaters, Charlie Chaplin traveled to the Ramova Theater to host the premiere of *The Great Dictator*. As for many movie theaters, TV (then VCRs), a changing neighborhood, and suburban sprawl brought the Ramova to a close in the late 1980s. In May 2005, a group of neighbors and preservationists formed Save the Ramova (www.savetheramova. com) to help preserve the structure. The **Ramova Grill** (3510 S. Halsted St., 773/847-9058) down the block serves diner grub and lots of chili at old-school prices (grilled cheese, $1.50; pork chop sandwich, $4.50).

STANDING LINCOLN
Lincoln Park at N. Dearborn Parkway
(1887)

hicago has more than its share of monumental tributes to the great political leaders of Illinois and beyond, and likely no other leader is as celebrated in stone as Abraham Lincoln. One of those statues, *Standing Lincoln*, is not only the city's oldest public statue, its history is surrounded by artistic triumph, intrigue, and scandal.

The monument stands at the foot of Lincoln Park, just south of the Chicago History Museum, in an area full of posh mansions and tree-lined walkways. The statue was designed by the noted sculptor Augustus Saint-Gaudens, who used Lincoln's 1860 life mask as a model. Although the statue is a realistic portrayal of Lincoln, it does not depict his modest beginnings as a wood splitter or his career as a Springfield lawyer. Instead, standing erect with an intent stare, beard and eyebrows bristling, Saint-Gaudens's Lincoln has the bearing of a Greek or Roman god. Stanford White designed the open, white stone spaces and other details of the monument, elevating the mood and enhancing the image of Lincoln alone. He placed the statue of Lincoln in the center of a classical circular pedestal.

Lincoln's grandson, also named Abraham Lincoln, unveiled the statue on October 22, 1887, and Leonard Swett gave the commemorative address. Leonard Swett was a friend from Lincoln's days in Springfield; Lincoln biographer Alexander McClure noted that "Of all living men, Leonard Swett was the one most trusted by Lincoln." Yet Swett's business affairs were mired in corruption. Rumors of his illegal deals and swindling associates became a political embarrassment to Lincoln. Later, Swett worked as an attorney for the Lincoln estate and helped to organize and conduct a hearing that confined Mary Todd Lincoln to an insane asylum.

The monument's architect, Stanford White, was an even more controversial figure. As the designer of New York's first Madison Square Garden, Vanderbilt Mansion, and the Astors' Mansion, he was the most noted designer of his era. White was even more famous for his womanizing than his architecture. He invented "the red velvet swing," from which he courted young women. White hung the swing in the den of his tower apartment in Madison Square Garden. He claimed the swinging motion served as an aphrodisiac for his female guests. One of the women White seduced was actress Evelyn Nesbit, whom he had met when she was just 16 years old. While watching a play at Madison Square Garden, White was shot by Nesbit's jealous, millionaire husband, Harry K. Thaw. The incident and resulting trial were depicted in the book, film, and theatrical versions of E. L. Doctorow's *Ragtime*. White was portrayed in the film version by Norman Mailer.

During the 1960s, the statue became a memorable backdrop for anti-war protesters. After meeting in the Old Town neighborhood near North and Wells, hippies marched to Lincoln Park, where they were tear gassed by police and routed towards the statue.

As the statue stands on the Chicago History Museum grounds, it's easy to combine a visit to both for a perfect Chicago afternoon.

☞ *LINCOLN STANDING* STANDS ON THE grounds of the **Chicago History Museum** (1601 N. Clark St., 312/642-4600), known as the Chicago Historical Society until 2006. Museum or society, it contains over 22 million artifacts related to Chicago's history. These include Abraham Lincoln's deathbed, artifacts from local Native American tribes, period clothing, furniture, artwork, tools, automobiles, and architectural details from Chicago's most famous buildings. The museum also features a bookstore, photo and document archive, lectures, films, photo exhibits, tours, and dozens of other annual events celebrating Chicago's history.

OLDEST LIQUOR DISTRIBUTOR

 HOUSE OF GLUNZ
1206 N. Wells Street
(1888)

Filled with dusty, antique bottles of brandy, whiskey from World War I, and Depression-era beer containers, the House of Glunz looks more like a museum dedicated to liquor than a thriving business. But thriving it is, and thriving it has been since 1888.

"My great grandfather started the business," Chris Donovan begins. "Before that he worked at a downtown area brewery owned by Charles Wacker. His friend and neighbor, Oscar Mayer, had already established his meat packing business, so with the urging and help of Wacker and Mayer, he began selling beer in what was then the far North Side."

Chicago's Old Town neighborhood is filled with bronze plaques and markers documenting the lives of Old Town residents like Wacker, Mayer, and Dr. Scholl. Today, these men are known as both legendary figures and brand names. But in 1879, at the time Glunz arrived from Westphalia, Germany, they were all young businessmen transforming Chicago from a burnt-out cinder into the third largest city in the nation.

Much of the city's early fortune relied on the railroads and heavy industry, the large German and Irish populations, proximity to water from Lake Michigan, and grain from the West. These resources also made Chicago the beer and brewing capital of the nation. Wacker made his early fortune brewing beer, and Glunz began working for him as a deliveryman in 1880. "My great grandfather started by delivering beer throughout downtown and the North Side by horse-drawn wagons in wooden barrels," Donovan says.

Glunz's hard work and loyalty were rewarded in 1888 when Wacker and Mayer loaned him the money to set up his own distributorship. Glunz maintained a relationship with his mentor, and in 1893 Wacker arranged for Glunz to become Chicago's distributor of Schlitz Beer. That was also the same year as the Columbian Exposition, one of the world's largest events. Wacker pulled some strings to get Glunz a choice spot there, which meant as much to him then as the Taste of Chicago means to Chicago's restaurants today.

The rest, they say, is history. At what is now 1208 North Wells Street, Glunz opened a bar, where he served sandwiches and bottled beer in the basement. He sold beer, wine, and spirits through World War I. The family line maintains that House of Glunz survived Prohibition by making sacramental wines. After the war and into the television age, Glunz continued as the North Side and suburban distributor for Schlitz. With slogans like, "When you're out of Schlitz, you're out of beer," Schlitz was the nation's top local and national beer throughout much of the 1940s, 1950s, and 1960s.

The business eventually outgrew its location and moved to 7100 North Capitol Drive in Lincolnwood. In 1993, Glunz's three grandsons, Louis III, John, and Joseph divided the business among their 93 children and grandchildren. Barbara Glunz-Donovan and her son Chris have transformed this blue-collar, sawdust-on–the-floor tavern into a posh winery and fine liquor emporium. The rear portion of the House of Glunz features a semi-private tasting room lined with wooden panels. Liquor connoisseurs from around the world travel to Glunz to sample and buy liquor at prices as large as a down payment for a house. "Some of the rarer products we sell include Joseph Etournaud Brandy from 1895, a Spey Royal single malt scotch with a tax stamp of 1934, and Empress Josephine Brandy from 1811 that sells for $8,000 a bottle," Donovan elaborates.

Hosting events like wine tastings and lectures, the House of Glunz remains an important part of neighborhood life. In this way the business has changed along with the neighborhood— but hey, what's wrong with a little change every hundred years or so?

👉 BACK IN THE 1880S WHEN THE HOUSE of Glunz opened, the area near Wells and Division streets (Old Town) was largely a German settlement, which meant beer and taverns abounded. This tradition was upheld by the 43rd Ward's longtime alderman (1933–1967), Paddy Bauler. Weighing over 300 pounds and also a saloon keeper, Bauler presided over an empire of graft and corruption from his headquarters in a bar located at North and Sedgwick avenues. He is famous for his quote, "Chicago ain't ready for reform." Perhaps it is this freewheeling heritage that would establish Old Town as Chicago's counterculture headquarters in the 1960s. Jazz clubs featured Miles Davis, and folk clubs featured Bob Dylan and Pete Seeger.

"It was the folk boom that made Old Town happen," said Peter Amft, a photographer whose credits include hundreds of books, albums covers, magazine spreads, and being tapped by Mick Jagger to be the official photographer for the Rolling Stones's 1972 tour. "Clubs like the Fickle Pickle, Mother Blues, the Blind Pig, and the Gate of Horn attracted people like Dylan, Judy Collins, and later Janis Joplin to perform in the area. An atmosphere began to develop. One person with long hair and a guitar would sit on a fire hydrant and start playing. Another musician would chime in, and pretty soon you had a hootenanny."

The music led to a countercultural explosion. Hare Krishnas wandered the streets in orange robes, burning incense. Alternative businesses lined the streets—head shops like Bazaar Bazaar, a structure the size of an indoor parking garage completely devoted to selling bongs, rolling papers, black light posters, and psychedelic lights. Attractions like Ripley's Believe It or Not Museum and The Wax Museum brought in tourists. And, so did the strip clubs, with silhouettes of nude and semi-nude dancers, shadowed by lights of changing colors (à la the beginning of the James Bond films), preening in the windows.

"It was a destination. I mean you would walk down the street and see Mike Bloomfield dragging a guitar case, Mama Cass visiting Mother Blues, Janis Joplin stopping someone on the street, asking for a light," Amft says. "It was a bohemian atmosphere where you could see other people with long hair, a place where you could fly your freak flag, a carnival of sights, a place that doesn't exist anymore."

Gradually, Old Town was filled with more tourists gawking at hippies than hippies. Local residents put up signs saying, "Suburbanites Go Home." The strip clubs multiplied and turned into peep show houses and adult book stores. The genie was out of the bottle and the air began to smell. As the 60s turned into the 70s and disco lights replaced folk clubs, the hippie days of Old Town became a thing of the past. If you are looking for a bar where the hippie feel has been somewhat preserved, try the **Old Town Ale House** (219 W. North Ave., 312/944-7020).

 DALEY'S RESTAURANT
809 E. 63rd Street
(1892)

t is a busy Monday morning, and as the customers at Daley's Restaurant dine on plates of scrambled eggs, salmon patties, smothered pork chops, and grits, they do so in the shadow of the 63rd Street stop of the Jackson Park 'L.' As you look at the old black and white photographs of the Columbian Exposition and the iron engines of the Southside Electric Railroad that line Daley's Restaurant's walls, and then peer back at the white steel beams of the 'L,' it isn't hard to imagine what the street must have been like shortly before 1892.

Chicago's Southeast Side was practically a new city. The University of Chicago, the rapid transit line, and the structures for the Columbian Exposition were all being built. If, in 1872, Chicago was reborn like a Phoenix from the ashes, the Columbian

Exposition was the city's coming out party. A couple of years earlier, John Daley was working on the rail line. Tired of lifting steel I-beams in the cold Chicago winds, he began to operate a food wagon for the workers.

"Old man Daley followed the 'L' workers with a restaurant on a carriage," says Nick Zarouchliotis, who currently owns and manages Daley's. "He was cooking for them for two years, but when the Columbian Exposition took place in 1892 he figured it was time to stop moving and he rented this spot." Even after the 27 million visitors who had attended the fair had gone, Daley's Restaurant continued to prosper.

"At that time the park [Jackson Park] was all filled in where before there had just been water," Zarouchliotis—everyone calls him "Nick Z"—said. "The restaurant was only about one third the size of the place, but it was enough to feed the workers. The area was a mix of Irish, German, and Jewish. Daley's served items like sandwiches, corned beef, eggs and hash, a lot of the items we still have now."

Just as he foresaw the future in 1892, John Daley once again peered into his crystal ball. "In 1918 old man Daley bought oil wells in Texas, and he did so well that he sold the place to my uncle's father, Tom Kyros. He emigrated here from Greece before the turn of the century and was working here as a waiter when he and another Greek guy (Paul Emmanuel) took over in 1918."

A fire temporarily closed the restaurant in the 1920s, but the restaurant was rebuilt.

"Back then there still weren't a lot of cars and trucks," Zarouchliotis says. "Oscar Mayer brought ham and bacon in on a wagon from his slaughterhouse at 43rd Street, and people like the 'egg man' brought eggs, and the 'milk man' brought milk, and since there was no refrigeration the 'ice man' had to come around at least twice a day with giant chunks of ice, which he carried across the street using steel tongs. During the Great Depression we used to go to farms in Indiana to buy meat right from the farmers."

The restaurant's website also relates how the partners wanted to expand in 1932, but just after the old building was demolished and the foundation was laid, the Washington Park National Bank, also at 63rd and Cottage Grove, failed. Kyros went to work at Deppie Baking Co. and Emmanuel at Power's Cafeteria until 1937, when they had saved up enough to completely rebuild the restaurant.

The Great Depression soon ended, and during the 1940s and 50s the area around Daley's was like "Rush Street South." It was close to the train lines and, eventually, the Dan Ryan Expressway and Lake Shore Drive. It teemed with nightclubs, bars, and what may have been the South Side's greatest movie palace, Chicago's Tivoli Theater (not to be confused with the Tivoli which still exists in Downers Grove—see Oldest [suburban] Movie Theater, p. 230), just south of the southeast corner of 63rd Street and Cottage Grove Avenue between the Strand Hotel and the Cinderella Ball Room. When the Chicago Tivoli Theater opened in 1921, its owners, Balaban and Katz, built it to rival the Riviera Theater on the North Side and the Chicago Theater downtown. Patterned after the Chapel of Versailles, it could seat over 3,400 people.

As Zarouchliotis walks through the Daley Restaurant, he points to pictures of customers that line the walls—entertainers like Sam Cooke, Moms Mabley, Red Foxx, and Richard Pryor; boxers Muhammad Ali and Joe Frazier; and politicians like mayors Harold Washington, Eugene Sawyer, and Richard J. Daley, and Richard M. Daley.

"A lot of famous people came in here in the 1940s and 50s, but in the 1960s and early 70s we had some rough years," Zarouchliotis says. "The Tivoli was taken down in 1963, and a lot of other

businesses left. Then it got rougher. The headquarters for the
Blackstone Rangers [an infamous street gang of the 1960s and
70s] was not far away, at Stony and 63rd."

There was also a change in personnel. In 1960 Emmanuel
went back to Greece, and in 1965, Kyros retired after 47 years.
Tom's son, George Kyros, and his nephew George Potakis carried Daley's through the hard times. Although the restaurant
had always featured hearty gravies and workingman's foods,
soul food staples like grits, catfish, yams, greens, and others
were added to the menu. In 1990 Zarouchliotis took over, and
today Nick and his son Alex run the restaurant. Aside from the
soul food, the menu, which offers meat loaf, roast tom turkey,
liver with onions, t-bone steaks, and half-spring chickens, probably hasn't changed much since John Daley opened it in 1892.
The prices may be a little higher, but with almost all dinners
under ten dollars, Daley's still fits the working person's budget.
Just as it's done for almost 120 years, the 'L' still rumbles by at
regular intervals. To the northeast, the Museum of Science and
Industry is still a marvel; to the northwest, students still study
at the University of Chicago. Alas, the Columbian Exposition is
gone.

*Many may comment that the Berghoff Restaurant is missing from this
book. In fact, the idea for this book was partially inspired by the extensive media coverage and local attention the closing of the Berghoff
received. However, I, like many Chicagoans, believe the Berghoff's current incarnation is so different from the original that is not the same
establishment.*

THE COLUMBIAN EXPOSITION OF 1893 attracted over 27 million people from all over the world during its six month reign. Inventions that were introduced at the fair include the mainstream use of electricity, the moving picture, the Ferris wheel, and the largest building ever constructed. Visitors included kings, queens, dukes, duchesses, President Grover Cleveland, Henry Ford, Thomas Edison, George Westinghouse, Frank Lloyd Wright, Walt Disney Sr., and *Wizard of Oz* writer Frank L. Baum, who modeled his Emerald City after the fair. In short, it might have been the greatest gathering of not only the nineteenth century, but of any century.

Over one hundred years later, little remains of the massive fairgrounds, but you can still see evidence of this great event. The most prominent, of course, is the **Museum of Science and Industry**. Located at 57th Street and Lake Shore Drive (773/684-1414, www.msichicago.org), it was built as the Palace of Fine Arts and the only permanent structure in the fair. Today it is one of the largest museums in the world, housing classic attractions beloved by generations of Chicagoans like the Coal Mine, the U-505 Submarine, the Apollo 8 space capsule, and a nineteenth-century streetscape, alongside exhibits devoted to the latest scientific developments.

Another remnant of the exposition is the **Statue of the Republic**. Located at the south end of Jackson Park near Oak Woods Cemetery, it is a 65-foot golden figure of a woman holding a globe and an eagle. The statue welcomed the almost 30 million visitors to the fair, facing what was then the Court of Honor.

Finally, the **Midway Plaisance** sits between 59th and 60th streets and joins Jackson and Washington parks between Cottage Grove and Stony Island avenues. During the fair it was known as "the avenue of sin." While the exposition housed many artistic and cultural exhibits, "the Midway" was predominantly known as the home of beer gardens, cigar dens, and exotic dancers doing the "hootchie coochie" from far away lands. That means, of course, it was the most popular attraction of the fair, and was largely responsible for the event turning a profit. Today it is a pleasant, grassy area filled with trees, wild birds, and squirrels. In past winters it was flooded for ice skating, and now it is mainly used for strolling, jogging, and studying by students and employees of the University of Chicago. The Midway Plaisance is the origin of the term "the midway" used at carnivals, as well as the moniker "the Monsters of the Midway" for the Chicago Bears.

OLDEST SKYSCRAPER

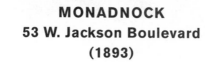

MONADNOCK
53 W. Jackson Boulevard
(1893)

The tragedy of the Chicago Fire had one positive impact: the rubble-filled city provided a blank slate for a new generation of urban planners and architects. These designers transformed Chicago from a fever-infested prairie town to a city with some of the most beautiful buildings in the world. One of the leading revolutionary structures to emerge at this time was the Monadnock building.

Located at 53 West Jackson Boulevard, the 17-story building is 197 feet tall. By today's standards, it is a middleweight among giants. In 1890, however, Chicago's tallest buildings seldom exceeded six stories. The area of the Loop from State Street west to the Chicago River was nothing more than a group of one-story structures and riverfront shacks. The Monadnock dominated downtown.

The northern half of the building, designed by Burnham and Root, was erected using load-bearing construction. In other words, the walls at the base had to be six feet thick in order to support the weight of the rest of the structure. While under construction, advanced, steel-framed technology came to the forefront of building design. Instead of tearing the building down and starting again, Holabird and Roche designed a southern half, which implemented steel-framed construction and allowed for a narrower base with supporting walls and larger windows.

In 1893, the Monadnock was called "an achievement unsurpassed in architectural history." Louis Sullivan described the building as "an amazing cliff of brickwork, rising sheer and stark, with subtlety of line and surface, a direct singleness of purpose that gives the thrill of romance. It was the first and last word of its kind."

Inside, the building is no less spectacular. The lobby and the interior hallways contain window frames, mantles, and trim of solid oak and varnished in a bright, blonde tone. Portions of the floors feature hand-cut, one-quarter-inch tiles, painstakingly laid out in beautiful patterns. The staircase railings are black wrought iron, rivaling any balcony in New Orleans, with handrails of solid oak and stairs of white granite. Large, open windows and skylights provide an openness and brightness unprecedented in the late 1800s.

Today, the building houses over three hundred suites, as well as a bank, three restaurants, a flower shop, and other businesses. The Monadnock was placed on the National Register of Historic Places in 1970 and designated a Chicago landmark in 1973. The building is not only a monument to Chicago architecture, but an important milestone in the history of architecture.

☞ BUILT WITHIN A CORRIDOR THAT REVOLU-
tionized architecture after the Great Chicago Fire,
the Monadnock building is surrounded by other architectural
wonders of the nineteenth century. Most notable of these is the
Rookery (209 S. La Salle St.), named after a structure built after
the Chicago Fire that served as both a temporary City Hall and
a favorite nesting spot for birds (1888). The building itself is a
combination of masonry and skeletal forms; each aspect of the
building has provided an example for future architects to follow.
Its most distinguishing feature has to be the atrium/lobby. Designed by Frank Lloyd Wright in 1905, the large, open skylights
exemplify both the beauty and the functionality of Prairie School
design. Also nearby is the **Fisher Building** (343 S. Dearborn
Ave.), built in 1896. It is a slim, Gothic tower, best known for the
various figures that decorate the outside, including eagles and
mythical beasts. The exterior, atrium, and interior lobby carry an
aquatic theme, their terra cotta and plaster fish, seashells, and
mythical sea creature decorations seeming to poke fun at the
building's name. The Rookery and Fisher Building are open to the
public and can be investigated as you wish. Formal tours are also
conducted by groups like the **Chicago Architecture Foundation** (312/922-3432).

OLDEST REFERENCE LIBRARY

NEWBERRY LIBRARY
Walton and Clark streets
(1893)

Do you want to play scholar for a day? Then put on your tweed jacket and walk into the ivy-covered brownstone known as the Newberry Library. You can reference some of America's greatest collections in Native American history, cartography, and the humanities; the personal papers of author Sherwood Anderson and journalist and screenwriter Ben Hecht; and many other wonderful and interesting things.

Established in 1893, the same year as the Chicago Public Library, the Newberry Library has been a center for cultural, academic, and scholarly activities for over one hundred years. The original Chicago Public Library building at Randolph Street and

Michigan Avenue is no longer housing books, but the Newberry Library thrives as Chicago's oldest reference library.

The roots of the Newberry go back to 1841, when Walter Newberry established a reading room. "Newberry earned his fortune in banking, railroads, and especially real estate, where he 'bought by the acre and sold by the foot'," Richard Brown, Senior Research Fellow at the Newberry Library and a Newberry Library historian, explains. "He left his considerable estate to his daughters with the provision that if there was not an heir that the money was to be used to establish a free public library. His daughters did not marry and, with the death of his widow in 1885, the movement to start a library began."

Within eight years, the brownstone was built. Designed by architect Henry Ives Cobb (who also built the structure now housing the Excalibur Nightclub), it was placed in what was then the center of the city. "With Washington Park Square right across the street, and its proximity to what was then the State Street and Clark Street street car lines, the location was very accessible to the public," according to Brown.

The Newberry currently holds a collection of 1.5 million books, five million manuscript pages, and three hundred thousand maps. "The library is devoted to the humanities, including history, arts, literature, music, philosophy, art, and other aspects of the humanities," Brown says. "We are ranked second behind the British Library with printing, tied with the Smithsonian as far as the history of Native Americans is concerned, and also have large collections devoted to the Renaissance, twentieth century history until World War II, and a large collection in cartography."

The Newberry also offers a variety of programs, including adult education classes and seminars, book discussions and meet-the-author programs, photo restoration services, and genealogy services, including family research arranged by surname and place name, Chicago genealogy databases, and internet genealogy services.

☞ THE NEWBERRY LIBRARY IS NEAR THE bars and restaurants of Rush Street, which are frequented by thousands and can be found in most tourist directories. One offbeat historic site that guidebooks probably won't mention is the **Valley of Chicago's Scottish Rite Cathedral** (929 N. Dearborn St.). The Valley of Chicago (an order of the Freemasons) was formerly housed at 293–5 North Dearborn Street from 1900 to 1911. In 1911, the order acquired the property known as Medinah's Mosque, built in 1867 in a Gothic Revival style. Everything except for the limestone walls were destroyed by the Great Chicago Fire in 1871. Dankmar Adler was hired to restore the structure, and his success in that job was said to have launched his architectural career.

CENTRAL CAMERA COMPANY
230 S. Wabash Avenue
(1899)

"The camera started as a wet plate in the 1830s," Albert D. Flesch, current president of Central Camera, instructs. "Both the French and English claim credit for its invention, but most people in America were not really introduced to photography until after the Civil War, when Mathew Brady's photos of President Lincoln and the battle scenes of the Civil War appeared. At that time the photographic process involved moving one or usually two large carts filled with cameras, tripods, and all of the silver nitrate and other chemicals necessary in the plate development process to the location." A day of shooting in the field might yield only a few photographic plates. To change this, George Eastman introduced the roll film camera in the 1880s. "They were large and awkward, and cost two dollars," Flesch says. "After the film was shot the camera had to be sent back to Kodak, which developed the film and reloaded the camera. That cost one dollar, and at that time a loaf of bread was a nickel, so it was very expensive."

Since 1899, the Flesch family and Central Camera Company have seen the art of photography develop from the Kodak roll cameras to digital machines. "My grandfather came here from a Jewish section of Hungary near Romania," Flesch says. "At first he worked at a store downtown called Siegel Cooper. In 1894 they asked him to work in the photo department." A meticulous man with an interest in the arts and the process of machinery, he saw the future in what was to become the multi-billion dollar camera business. "In the early days of the automobile, Henry Ford saw the car not only as something that can move you from here to there, but as an outlet to help let you do whatever you wanted to do," Flesch says. "Whether it was a photo of a general or a family picnic, my grandfather saw the future of the camera not as an expensive toy for the rich, but a way to capture and remember one's personal history. In this way, he invested not only in machines, but in people's minds, and how they came to view photography and photos as a continuous part of their lives."

In 1899, Flesch opened Central Camera at 31 East Adams Street. Flesch was not only in an entirely new field, but also had to argue with the Eastman Kodak Company, who claimed a monopoly on the photographic industry. Kodak's power in the industry was strengthened even more with the development of the Brownie box camera, which was lighter and far more portable than previous models. "My grandfather was continually involved in disagreements from the early 1900s until about 1912," Flesch shares. "At that time they would tell the dealers that if you sell our products you could not sell anybody else's products. Because of this my grandfather's store must have closed 10 to 12 times."

Central Camera remained at 31 East Adams from 1899 until 1907. In 1907, the company moved to the first store north of the Palmer House on Wabash, where it remained until 1929 when the hotel was evacuated and torn down so that a new building could be constructed. The store then moved about two hundred yards south to 230 South Wabash. "We moved to our current location in February of 1929. We did it by hiring 50 people who passed the small boxes down a line like a human train." The stock market crashed only months later, and Central Camera struggled through the Great Depression. Often the store's deposits were as little as $15 a day. During this period, Harold R. Flesch and Stanley J. Flesch joined their father at the store.

Even though the economy slowed down, the refinement of the camera sped up. "In 1923 a man named Barnack was trying to invent a new prototype for the motion picture camera," Flesch says. "In order to have the film advance faster he designed a type of spool with notches in it, which eventually became the prototype for a roll with 10 to 20 exposures." In Europe, the Germans, English, and Swiss improved the lenses and optics of cameras, resulting in such models as the Exacta, Leica, and Zeiss. George Eastman, who named his company after Kodiak bears, incorporated this improved technology into his cameras. Over time, cameras also became smaller and more portable. In the late 1940s, Edwin Land developed the Polaroid, which used a patented chemical process to create finished, positive black-and-white print in minutes. Says Flesch, "My father, Harold R. Flesch, who died in 1983, was able to experience all these changes, from the sheet film camera and plate cameras and the single shot Brownie through the built-in light meters, advanced motors, and auto exposure cameras."

The current owner, Albert D. Flesch says, "I began working here during summers in 1961 and '62, and came here full time after college in '68. There were many retail camera stores, as many as 16 or 17, throughout the Loop."

In the 1990s digital photography took hold of the market. A photographer once needed to know how to use f-stops and light meters, how to focus, and usually how to develop photos in a darkroom. Now, anyone can "point and click" and cameras are sold in large electronics stores. Flesch says that Central Camera Company has survived this change by staffing knowledgable people who love photography and by remaining competitively priced. Now in its third generation, it has remained a Loop fixture not by being a slave to technology, but by honing the art of photography's past and present and serving the whole spectrum of customers. Central Camera may soon be owned by a fourth generation from the Flesch family, as Albert D. Flesch's children, Rai and Shira, have been working in the store part time.

☞ CAMERAS ARE WONDERFUL, MECHANICAL objects. But even more fantastic are the images they create. Located just two blocks west of Central Camera, the **Art Institute of Chicago** (111 S. Michigan Ave., 312/443-3600) has acquired one of the most extensive photo collections in the world. Spanning from the art's beginnings in the 1830s to today's digital works, the collection currently displays a wide variety of pieces from the stark, urban scenes of Berenice Abbott and Harry Callahan to the wilderness landscapes of Ansel Adams. For fans of the avante garde, the surreal photos of Richard Avedon and the European masterworks of Brassai are just a few highlights. Many of these are part of in the permanent collection. Others can be viewed by special appointment.

II. Food, Fun, and Entertainment

OLDEST AFRICAN-AMERICAN NEWSPAPER

CHICAGO DEFENDER
200 S. Michigan Avenue
(1905)

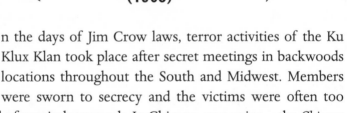

In the days of Jim Crow laws, terror activities of the Ku Klux Klan took place after secret meetings in backwoods locations throughout the South and Midwest. Members were sworn to secrecy and the victims were often too afraid of reprisals to speak. In Chicago, one voice—the *Chicago Defender*—brought these tragedies to the attention of the rest of the nation

The *Chicago Defender* was founded in 1905 by Robert S. Abbott and produced in a kitchen, with three hundred 25-cent copies cranked out on a small press. After five years, however, Abbott realized the need for an African-American-run newspaper nationwide. Following the lead of black militants like Marcus Garvey, the *Chicago Defender* began to not only report on issues relating to African-Americans in Chicago, but throughout the South. Abbott described lynchings and beatings in vivid detail, and drawings, often in red ink, illustrated the point even further. Words like negro or black were not used. Instead, African-Americans were referred to as "the race."

The Underground Railroad transported slaves to freedom through a series of safe houses before the Civil War, and the *Chicago Defender* used similar methods to spread its message many years later. Passed along by Pullman porters, musicians, cobblers, and salesmen who traveled by mule-driven wagons throughout the South, the *Chicago Defender* was often the only uncensored media outlet for African-Americans. Organizations like the Ku Klux Klan soon realized this. KKK members confiscated the paper from anyone caught reading it and often severely beat them for it.

These tactics only heightened the legitimacy and importance of the newspaper. The *Chicago Defender* was read under shady trees, at meetings of sharecroppers, in churches, in barbershops, and in general stores. It is believed that each paper was passed around to as many as five people, giving it an estimated circulation of five hundred thousand people each week. During World War I, the paper was a beacon for the African-American migration to Chicago, as well as other northern cities like Gary, Indiana, and Detroit, Michigan.

In July 1919, an African-American boy named Eugene Williams drowned at 29th Street beach. It was not an accident, however. The boy drowned after being stranded on a railroad tie, afraid to come to shore because angry whites were throwing bricks and stones from a pier. His crime: accidentally swimming into the "white" part of the beach. The perpetrators were not arrested. The five days of burning, looting, and hysterical beatings that followed turned entire neighborhoods into war zones. At the end of the five days of rioting, 23 blacks and 15 whites were dead, and almost three hundred people were wounded.

The September 2, 1919, issue of the *Chicago Defender* described one of the scenes: "Excitement ran high all through the day July 28. Groups of men whose minds were inflamed by rumors of brutal attacks on men, women and children crowded the public thoroughfares in the South Side district from 27th to 39th streets. Some were voicing sinister sentiments, others gesticulating, and the remainder making their way home to grease up the old family revolver. Added to the already irritable feeling was the fact that some whites had planned to make a fore day visit to the South Side homes with guns and torches. This message was conveyed to a group of men who were congregated near 36th and State streets. Provident Hospital at 36th and Dearborn streets, situated in the heart of the 'black belt,' as well as other hospitals in the surrounding districts, are filled with the maimed and dying. Every hour, every minute, every second finds patrols backing up and unloading the human freight branded with the red symbol of this orgy of hate. So pressing has the situation become that schools, drug stores and private houses are being used. Trucks, drays and hearses are being used for ambulances."

Throughout the 1920s and 1930s the *Chicago Defender* printed stories of racial incidents such as this, as well as descriptions of the frequent lynchings and beatings that occurred throughout the South. John H. Sengstacke purchased the *Chicago Defender* in 1940, and kept it a voice for African-American issues. It is one of the chief sponsors of Chicago's annual Bud Billiken Day Parade, the African-American counterpart to the St. Patrick's Day Parade, Columbus Day Parade, and other parade events organized by Chicago's ethnic communities. The publication began to be published on a daily basis in 1954. The *Chicago Defender* provided firsthand reporting of the civil rights movement and helped to spread the message of African-American leaders like Martin Luther King, Jr. and Malcolm X. Sengstacke served as publisher until his death in May 1997.

In 2008, the paper once again became the *Chicago Weekly Defender*. The change to a weekly format is part of the paper's overall modernization and expansion plan that should allow it to double its circulation from fifty thousand to one hundred thousand, as well as allow the paper to enter the Wisconsin, Iowa, and Northwest Indiana markets.

The paper's longtime headquarters at 3455 South Indiana Avenue was designated a Chicago landmark in 1998. A former Jewish synagogue, it was designed by architect Henry Newhouse in 1899 and is part of Chicago's Bronzeville Historic District.

THE BRONZEVILLE NEIGHBORHOOD WAS once known as the cultural center of African-American Chicago, with figures like Louis Armstrong and Gwendolyn Brooks re-defining art and American culture. Ironically, **Stephen A. Douglas**, the man who debated Lincoln for the 1860 election, is buried in a State Historic Area (636 E. 36th St.), not far from the original office of the *Chicago Defender*. Douglas was known for supporting both the Kansas–Nebraska Act that would let the new territories decide for themselves whether or not they wanted to permit slavery, and the Dred Scott Supreme Court decision, which said that people of African descent who were held as slaves could never become U.S. citizens. He later changed his position, encouraging Illinois to join the Union in the Civil War. He died shortly before the war started. Efforts for a Douglas memorial began in 1866, but the site was not completed until 1881. His grave is marked by a 96-foot tall granite pillar with a 9-foot bronze statue of Douglas at the top, overlooking Lake Michigan. The base is a Vermont marble mausoleum that holds Douglas's remains. Open areas around the tomb can be visited at any time.

OLDEST BATHHOUSE

DIVISION STREET RUSSIAN & TURKISH BATHS
1916 W. Division Street
(1906)

It's all about the sauna. While most saunas are 8' x 8' birch boxes with an electric-coil heater (in other words, a giant hot plate), the Division Street Russian Baths feature a huge 20' x 20' room heated by a brick oven that radiates over huge granite plates.

"We usually start the fire early in the morning," Joe Colucci, son of the baths' owner, explains. "Once we get it going, the oven is so strong that the granite usually stays hot the rest of the day." The starting of the fire is just part of the sauna ritual. Once the room is hot, dozens of men saunter into the three-leveled chamber. Some are naked, others wear towels, and some wear a white cotton garment that resembles a diaper. Once inside, these massive, often tattooed men take a plastic liquid laundry container that has been cut in half. They begin tossing water onto the "coals." As the granite sizzles, giant clouds of hot steam drift across the sauna, raising the temperature to almost two hundred degrees. The men take turns lying face down on the bench and getting their backs brushed with branches of oak leaves. After a few more minutes in the top heat, they run out into the shower area. Expletives echo through the chambers as the naked men hurl themselves into a large pool of water that is barely above 35 degrees. Then it is back into the sauna to repeat the ritual as many as four or five times before a final shower.

The baths, housed in a giant limestone building, opened in 1906. As Henrik Ibsen wrote in his play *Enemy of the People*, bathhouses were not used as escapes from the Chicago cold or as a working man's spa. They were a necessity to public health. "At that time few people in Chicago had running water, let alone hot water, let alone a bath or shower," Colucci says. "This was the way people bathed."

According to Colucci, the neighborhood was comprised mainly of Jews of Russian origin. While many Russians still frequented the baths' in the 1940s, the neighborhood had become the hub of Chicago's Polish immigrant community. It was during this time that Nelson Algren visited the baths. It seems that little has changed since the baths' glory days, when writers like Algren and Saul Bellow frequented the baths. "Things are very elementary here," Bellow wrote in his novel *Humboldt's Gift*. "Down in these super-heated sellers all these Slavonic cavemen and wood demons with hanging laps of fat and legs of stone and lichens boil themselves and splash water on their heads by bucket, repeating an ancient ritual that may or not even still exist in their village in the Carpathians."

The structure remained a secret, ethnic Chicago tradition through 1974, when Colucci's grandfather purchased the baths. "He was a successful businessman and bought it more or less

as a hobby," Colucci says. "At that time there were two sepa-
rate facilities, and three days a week, we had women's days."
Even though the neighborhood fell into decline in the 1970s and
1980s—Colucci says they "had shootings right in back of here
on Crystal"—the baths remained. Nonetheless, celebrities like
Burt Reynolds, John and Jim Belushi, Steven Seagal, Mike Ditka, James Gandolfini, Russell Crowe, and Jesse Jackson began
visiting the baths. In 2000, Colucci's grandfather passed away,
and his father took over the business. By then, Division Street's
old Polish bars became the hangout for hip young singles, who
found the worn wooden floors, hand-painted beer signs, and
leaky bathroom sinks preferable over the white-washed chain
bars and restaurants of suburban America. Soon, however,
these old bars began to be replaced by newer, chic restaurants
that tried to retain the old tables and touches of the "old world"
while adding gourmet appetizers, micro-brewed beers, and hip-
hop DJs.

Inside the sauna, however, little has changed. After dousing
themselves with heat, steam, cold water, and soap, the bathers
dress in towels or robes and head upstairs to the lounge. Here,
they break out the pickled herring, dill cucumbers, borscht, rye
bread, sausage, and cheese. Oh yeah, and don't forget the beer
and vodka. Taken ice cold from a refrigerator behind the counter, the vodka is poured into plastic cups and washed down with
Czech beer. Then the men place chess and backgammon sets
on tables, and the talk in European tongues lasts well into the
afternoon. The club is open from eight in the morning until ten
at night. Your best bet, however, is to get there about ten a.m.,
just before the lunchtime crowd. Towels and rubber sandals are
provided, but if you have a pair of old flip-flops at home, it is
best to bring your own, as well as a sandwich or snack. The fee
for using the baths is $20, but for that amount, you leave feel-
ing like a new person, with some old-school lessons to boot.

Women can also enjoy the Division Street Baths—minus the grunting, sweaty, naked men—Monday through Friday, 11AM to 3 PM. Visit http://chicagorussiansauna.com to see new options for women.

☞ IN THE 1950S (THE HEYDAY OF THE DIVISION Street Baths), the area of West Division Street between Ashland and Damen teemed with urban life round-the-clock. Immortalized in Nelson Algren's novels *The Neon Wilderness* and *The Man With the Golden Arm*, as well as the photographs of Art Shay, "Polish Broadway," was an area where Polish and other Eastern European immigrants mixed with white migrants from the Appalachian region. Amidst street-level ethnic culture and in 24-hour taverns, blue-collar workers drank cheap beer and highballs and even—yes, it is true—participated in prostitution and gambling. After a long period of relative blight when the bars were almost empty, the area has filled up again, this time with designer boutiques, sushi bars, and trendy bars that cater to the young transplants that have migrated to the area, usually via a Big Ten university. Yet there are a few holdovers from the Algren era. The **Gold Star Bar** (1755 W. Division St., 773/227-8700) has been a fixture since the days of Prohibition and is the closest thing to an "old man's bar" in the area. From the faded, 1950s-era painted sign over the windows to the dark, worn out floors, the Gold Star Bar still offers $2 domestic beers and walls that have not been re-touched by the Home Depot generation. The **Rainbo Club** (1150 N. Damen Ave., 773/489-5999) is another relic from a past generation, where the crowd has changed from Algren-era beatniks to Obama-era hipsters.

OLDEST NIGHTCLUB

GREEN MILL
4802 N. Broadway Avenue
(1907)

 he recent movie *Chicago* won an Academy Award for its portrayal of gangsters, jazz, and Prohibition in the Windy City. If the walls of the Green Mill could talk, they would tell an even more dramatic story of Chicago.

Opened in 1907, the lounge first called Pop Morse's Roadhouse was a stopping point for thirsty visitors going to and from the many area cemeteries. In 1909 the establishment's name changed to the Green Mill Gardens. The nightspot became a ragtime-era favorite for the up-and-coming neighborhood soon to be known as Uptown. Not more than a few blocks up the street on Argyle, Essanay studios set up shop. It wasn't long before stars like Wallace Beery and "Broncho Billy" Anderson (but apparently not Charlie Chaplin) made the Mill a favorite place to hang out.

The Roaring Twenties were the golden age of Uptown. The Uptown Theatre, the Riviera, and the Aragon Ballroom became the type of all-night, high-class jazz-era dance joints portrayed in so many Busby Berkeley movies. After the shows, many of the jazzmen and big band players would saunter over to the Green Mill. Entertainers like Al Jolson, Sophie Tucker, and Eddie Cantor all graced the stage here. In the late 1920s, the biggest player in town, Al Capone, hung his hat there, too. His chief gunman, Jack "Machine Gun" McGurn (who many believe was one of the machine-gun triggermen at the St. Valentine's Day Massacre), took 25 percent ownership of the club.

Legend has it that the Rendezvous Café at Clark Street and Diversey Parkway made the mistake of offering Joe E. Lewis more money to sing there instead of at his usual Green Mill gig. Even after the owners of the Green Mill tried to strong-arm the singer, Lewis still insisted on performing at the Rendezvous. Robert Rudd, a former resident of the Surf Hotel, says he heard the old-time residents tell the story of Lewis: "They say they saw him come stumbling out of the elevator, his throat slit from ear to ear so that he would never sing again. They all thought he was dead. He just kept bleeding all over the carpet. Finally, they brought him upstairs and then to a hospital. It was a miracle he lived. He couldn't sing no more, but that didn't stop him. He became a comedian and packed them in, especially later on in Las Vegas. He was always known for his voice, which sounded raspy, like a voice box." This story inspired the Hollywood film starring Frank Sinatra, *The Joker Is Wild*.

During the 1970s, Uptown ceased being such an entertainment haven and became a gang-infested neighborhood. One by one, the Uptown Theatre, the Riviera, and others stopped bringing in big-name concerts and showing movies. But the Green Mill's new owner, Dave Jemilo, kept the historic lounge going. Regular performers like Brad Goode and Ed Peterson pulled in a new, younger Chicago jazz audience in the late 1980s. In an effort to bring in customers during slow nights, Marc Smith started the Uptown Poetry Slam. The event changed the entertainment landscape in Chicago, and today the Green Mill is a landmark. While other jazz rooms have closed, the Green Mill—with its glowing neon sign, round leather booths, and strong Manhattans—will stick around for another hundred years.

THE GREEN MILL IS LOCATED IN THE SHADow of the **Uptown Theatre** (4816 N. Broadway). Designed by Rapp and Rapp and opened in 1925 for the Balaban and Katz chain, the theater is over 46,000 square feet and has 4,381 seats. This makes it not only the largest theater in Chicago, but even larger than New York's Radio City Music Hall. The theater was closed in the early 1980s. Over the years, groups with varying intentions have attempted to preserve and restore the structure, since named to the National Register of Historic Places and designated a Chicago Landmark. These include the dedicated **Friends of the Uptown** (www.uptowntheatre.com), a group of neighbors, architecture and theater buffs, and local tradespeople who have volunteered their skills to help restore parts of the theater and prevent further deterioration. The theater has been designated an important link in re-vitalizing the Uptown entertainment district, but the future status of the Uptown is still undecided.

OLDEST FILM STUDIO

ESSANAY STUDIOS
1333–1345 N. Argyle Street
(1908)

In order to dodge the rights and licensing fees from Thomas Edison's original movie camera patents, movie studios were always changing location. New York was filled with Edison's agents, so studios' next logical location became Chicago. George K. Spoor and Gilbert "Broncho Billy" Anderson started Essanay Studios in 1908. (They named it after themselves—"Ess" for Spoor and "Ay" for Anderson.) "Anybody who made movies using Edison's equipment, like Essanay, was technically breaking the law, but nobody paid attention to it," Michael Figliulo, who briefly worked as a motorcycle stuntman for Mack Sennett at Essanay, says. "In California they had gunfights over this, and until the courts overruled the patents, the little guys like Sennett told everybody to keep things quiet."

Anderson had a small part in *The Great Train Robbery*, which is generally regarded as the first narrative film. Known as "the first cowboy star," he starred in and produced films at Essanay. He also developed other actors who became Hollywood legends. "Essanay had Charlie Chaplin working over there, and they made Wallace Beery, Ben Turpin, and Gloria Swanson into stars. They were all nothing at first. I think Swanson was a secretary and Turpin and Beery started out as janitors," recalls Figliulo.

Mack Sennett's Keystone Cops comedies, "Broncho Billy" westerns, and Chaplin's early films were all shot in this Uptown studio. Occasionally Lincoln Park would stand in for the forest, Foster Avenue beach for the desert, and Lake Michigan for the ocean. Legend also has it that Swanson and Beery were married on the studio lot.

In 1914, Chaplin, who disliked the cold weather in Chicago, left for the sunshine and higher pay of California. Beery, Swanson, and Turpin followed. Soon after, Essanay stopped producing films. The building housed Essanay Lighting for several decades. (Now located at 1346 North Branch Street, Essanay Lighting maintains the studio's ties to show business, providing camera cranes, dollies, par lights, booms, and just about everything else needed for filmmaking except the talent.) On March 26, 1996, the Argyle Street building was named a Chicago landmark. The building, with its famous Indian head logo, still stands and is currently the home of the bilingual Augustine College. The memory of Essanay Studios remains celebrated in numerous books, plays, and television documentaries about Chicago history.

For some, the memories of Essanay's glory days in silent pictures live on as well. "The Essanay era was a special time," Figliulo says. "You didn't have sound or color, so it took some special acting to get the story across. Guys like Ben Turpin were truly funny, and Wallace Beery was the kind of guy who would take in a stray dog or cat. Chaplin, he was a great actor, but a real son of a bitch. Even though he was making more than the president, he wouldn't give you a cigarette."

THE ESSANAY FILM STUDIO HAS LONG stopped producing films, but it is still located in a vital part of Chicago. It is three blocks north of both the **Green Mill** (see Oldest Nightclub, p. 106) and the **Uptown Theatre** (4816 N. Broadway). It is also one block west of Chicago's **Little Vietnam** (also known simply as "Argyle Street"), largely settled by Vietnamese refuges who came to Chicago after the Vietnam War (Argyle St. between Sheridan and Broadway). The area features dozens of restaurants, gift shops, bakeries, and grocery stores including **Pho 888** (1137 W. Argyle St., 773/907-8838) for Vietnamese noodles, **Silver Seafood** (4829 N. Broadway, 773/784-0668) Chinese restaurant, and the **Broadway Supermarket** (4879 N. Broadway, 773/334-3838), which features live seafood and hard-to-find Asian delicacies.

OLDEST BAKERY (NOW AN EMPIRE)

 POMPEI BAKERY
various locations
(1909)

In 1909, immigrants from Italy were settling what is now known as the Taylor Street neighborhood. Coming to a country where baked goods meant hard rolls and coffee cakes and dinner meant roast beef and potatoes, the Italians felt lost. Where could they get food from home, they wondered?

Luigi Davino solved this problem by opening a bakery on Loomis Avenue and Taylor Street. Since the bakery stood near Our Lady of Pompeii Church, he decided to call it Pompei Bakery. There, he and his wife, Carmella, baked the thick-crusted, chewy bread they used to eat in Italy. They cut thick slices of bread and covered them with tomato sauce and cheese—pizza!

After World War II, Taylor Street blossomed into a full-fledged Little Italy. Like the street scenes from *The Godfather*, the area was filled with pushcart vendors, fruit stands, flower shops, newsstands, restaurants, and Italian bakeries. Luigi and Carmella slowly turned the business over to their sons Alfonso, Ralph, Solly, and Rogie. During the 1960s, construction of the Eisenhower Expressway and University of Illinois at Chicago campus literally tore apart Italian Taylor Street. Many of Pompei Bakery's customers moved to the suburbs, which didn't make the situation any easier, but the bakery weathered these tough times.

The area revitalized in the 1980s and 1990s. Pompei, in its third generation, expanded to a more modern facility at 1531 West Taylor Street. Once a bakery that only sold bread, then a popular lunchtime joint for their signature pizza varieties, Pompei is now a full-service restaurant and a center for quality dining and Italian culture. The menu offers over 25 types of pizza, their famous "pizza strudel," and 40 other delicious specialties, including their beloved pizzacotto, a loaf of thin, crusty bread filled with Italian goodies. Pompei is now a mini-chain with locations in Schaumburg, Oakbrook Terrace, Lake View, Oak Park, and two outlets in the Loop. It's a far cry from the mom-and-pop store that opened on Loomis in 1909, but just as tasty.

☞ DURING THE 1920S, 30S, AND 40S, **TAYLOR Street** between Halsted Street and Western Avenue was an urban scene right out of the movies. Its sidewalks were filled with wooden produce stands and flowers, and the streets were filled with push carts, horse- and mule-drawn wagons, children playing stickball, and vendors with little stands selling heated cheese bread yelling, "ahhhh pizza." Neighbors knew neighbors and if you wanted someone you simply yelled their name out the window. The construction of the Kennedy and Eisenhower expressways and the building of the University of Illinois–Chicago literally tore the neighborhood apart. In recent years, however, the efforts of a few tough hangers-on and stalwarts in the Italian-American community have once again made Taylor Street a thriving ethnic center, larger, cleaner, and friendlier than New York's overrated Little Italy.

The area has always united around the **Our Lady of Pompei Church** (1224 W. Lexington St.). This was the case when Italian immigrants pitched in to build the structure in 1910–11, and with the newer crop of donors who helped revitalize and restore it beginning in the early 1990s. Longtime businesses and must-stops on a Chicago-Italian tour include **Mario's Lemonade** (1068 W. Taylor St., open May through October only) and the new-ish **National Italian American Sports Hall of Fame** (1431 W. Taylor St., 773/226-5566), which highlights the heroics of sportsmen like Mario Andretti, Rock Marciano, Dan Marino, Cammi Granato, and many more. Then, of course, there are the restaurants— *abudanza, abudanza!* The best known of these is **The Rosebud** (1500 W. Taylor St., 312/942-1117). It is here that patrons like Frank Sinatra, President William Clinton, Secretary of State Hillary Rodham Clinton, Dustin Hoffman, and many others have sampled the Cavatelli a la Rosebud, Chicken Vesuvio, lasagna, and giambotta.

OLDEST BAKERY (STILL A BAKERY)

 ROESER'S BAKERY
3216 W. North Avenue
(1911)

As Roeser's Bakery approaches one hundred years of operation, John Roeser II, III, and IV can take pride that the chances against a business succeeding through four generations are almost 99-1—and yet they have accomplished exactly that. When John Roeser I arrived in Chicago from Germany in 1905, he couldn't have had the slightest idea that his bakery would still be operating well into the twenty-first century.

"When my father came here in 1905, he opened a wholesale bakery on Wells and Chicago near where Carson's Ribs now is. It was a three-wagon business, basically baking bread for the hotels and restaurants downtown," says John Roeser II. "It was brutal work, especially in the summer," John Roeser III continues. "Not only did he have to bake all night, but when he was finished, he would have to package everything, load it into a horse drawn wagon, and deliver it all over downtown. Then he would have to go back to the shop, gather his supplies, clean up, and prepare for the next day."

John Roeser I opened a retail outlet at the current location, 3216 West North Avenue, in 1911. "He still put in a lot of 16-hour days, but at least he was able to get some sleep," Roeser III says. Before coming to Chicago, Roeser baked in his native Germany and received formal culinary training at several shops in London. His new store not only allowed him an occasional day of rest, but it also gave him the opportunity to create many of the pastries, pies, cakes, and rolls that he had been trained to prepare. "At that time the neighborhood was on the outskirts of the city, and was mostly German and Scandinavian," Roeser II says. "Dania Hall, one of the largest Danish clubs in the city, was right around the corner, so he was very busy making coffee cakes, rye bread, and German hard water rolls for what were mostly northern European customers."

"You also have to remember that it was a much, much different time," Roeser III says. "There were no preservatives, no large stores or supermarkets, and the only cooling people had was maybe an ice box. So customers went to the neighborhood bakery two and sometimes three times a day to get a sweet roll for breakfast, hard roll for lunch, and maybe a loaf of rye bread and cake for dinner and dessert."

In this way the business survived through its first 20 years. At a time when most establishments would be coasting, two events—the Great Depression and World War II—created new challenges. "After I graduated from high school I decided to work at dad's bakery for a year while I made up my mind about whether or not I wanted to go to college," Roeser II says. "Then the Depression came. We weren't as hard hit as other parts of the country or other neighborhoods, as a lot of people were able to hold on to their jobs, but things were still tough and we had to really lower prices in order to sell anything. Sweet rolls were two cents, bread nine cents, and coffee cakes were fifteen cents." On the heels of the Great Depression came World War II. Although more manufacturing jobs flooded an area that was filled with small factories, the government made it harder to fill the customer's needs by rationing shortening, sugar, and butter. "We changed a lot of the recipes, and Anheuser-Busch made a kind of syrup that would come in 55 gallon drums that we could substitute for sugar," Roeser II says.

In the 1960s, the city of Chicago and Roeser's Bakery went through another series of changes. Roeser III, who earned a degree in sociology from Drake University before joining the bakery, explains, "In the twentieth century in Chicago the city more or less grew under the concentric circle theory of planning. This states that you have a downtown area and rings of immigration growing outward. The rings closest to the downtown are generally the newest immigrants and those with the lowest incomes. As you move away from the city you get people with more and more money building larger homes." The city's early ethnic neighborhoods, Italian Taylor Street (Taylor and Halsted), Greektown (Jackson and Halsted), Chinatown (22nd and Cermak), and Maxwell Street (Roosevelt and Halsted) follow this pattern.

"When my grandfather moved out here in 1911, the street car stopped at Pulaski," Roeser III relates. "This area was filled with large homes, almost like the suburbs. But as the city grew, so did the circles, and in the 1960s there was no place for the newest immigrants, which were Puerto Rican, to go. So they came here." At first, the Roesers feared that the change in population would be the end for their bakery. In order to adjust, Roeser II went to Puerto Rico to see what kinds of baked goods the people were eating. In the long run, though, their fears were unfounded. "The Puerto Ricans are a very family-oriented people," Roeser II says. "Their social life revolves around family graduations, birthdays, and cotillions. So even though we may have sold fewer coffee cakes, our orders for special and custom-inscribed cakes skyrocketed." After receiving his college degree and working in the food industry for several leading corporations, Roeser III decided that he would work for the family business "because it was at a slower pace and because I wanted to."

In order to remain viable, Roeser's Bakery has to adapt to again. The once solidly Puerto Rican neighborhood is gentrifying. "In this century the concentric circles theory has more or less been reversed," Roeser III says. "Now the wealthier people want to live close to downtown Chicago and those who are starting out are moving to the outskirts of the city."

Another generation will have to confront these issues. John Roeser IV is planning to join the business and will soon take over for his father. "We told him there were plenty of opportunities in other areas, but he will have none of it," Roeser III says. "He has wanted to go into the bakery as soon as he could walk and talk, so that is the way it is going to continue."

ROESER'S BAKERY IS A LANDMARK IN THE Humboldt Park neighborhood. The jewel of this area is **Humboldt Park** (roughly bounded by North Ave., California Ave., Division St., and Kedzie Ave.) itself. The idea for the park came in 1869. It was laid out as part of the city's boulevard system, which connects Humboldt, Garfield, and Douglas parks. The neighborhood then was heavily German, so it was to be named after Baron Friedrich Heinrich Von Humboldt, a famous German scientist. Noted landscape architect Jens Jensen refined the park's look. A naturalist in the vein of Frank Lloyd Wright, he helped add a large system of lagoons. Linked by tall grass and natural fauna, it was known as an inland "prairie river." In 1928, a field house was constructed on the property. A large, Bohemian-type structure, it is now the center for many park programs and cultural events, many specifically serving the Puerto Rican community that has predominated in Humboldt Park for decades. After shopping at Roeser's, drop in one of the Puerto Rican eateries, especially for the lechón (whole-roasted suckling pig, its dry yet flavorful taste has made it a longtime staple at neighborhood festivals). Try **La Cocina Boricua de la Familia Galarza** (2420 W. Fullerton Ave., 773/235-7377) or **Papa's Cache Sabroso** (2517 W. Division St., 773/862-8313). Or, pick up some Caribbean groceries to accompany Roeser's rolls, breads, and pastries. Neighborhood favorites include **Puerto Rico Food & Liquors** (2559 W. Augusta Blvd., 773/342-2678) and **Armitage Produce** (3334 W. Armitage Ave., 773/486-8133).

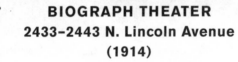

BIOGRAPH THEATER
2433–2443 N. Lincoln Avenue
(1914)

Many Chicagoans know that the Biograph Theater was the site where John Dillinger was killed in 1934. They may not know though that the theater had already been in existence for twenty years by then.

The Biograph Theater was built near the intersection of Lincoln, Fullerton, and Halsted in 1914. At that time, films were nothing more than a silent flicker on a stiff sheet. Movies were shunned by the middle, upper-middle, and upper classes, whose members preferred the sophistication of "legitimate theater." The movies' largest audiences were Russian, Italian, Greek, and German immigrants who didn't have such pretensions and also appreciated the lack of dialogue.

This all began to change when filmmaker D. W. Griffith joined Biograph Studios in the Bronx in 1912; Griffith revolutionized film, turning the formerly lower-class entertainment of immigrants into more of an acceptable art form for middle-class Americans. Although there was no connection to the New York–based studio, the Biograph Theater was named after the birthplace of the episodic film.

When the theater was conceived, most movie houses or "nickelodeons" were little more than storefront viewing areas with a few folding chairs. The Biograph changed much of this. While many movie theaters were merely converted from other buildings, noted classical architect Samuel Crowen designed the Biograph Theater specifically to be a theater. It contained the free-standing ticket booth and wide lobby that distinguished it from nickelodeons. To differentiate it from "legitimate theater" and advertise it with new audiences, the Biograph was given a grand, black and white marquee.

In the 1920s, many palatial movie houses were built downtown and throughout Chicago's neighborhoods. In fact, if it hadn't been for the famous night in July of 1934, the Biograph may have simply gone the way of hundreds of Chicago theaters. On that night the FBI, tipped off by the infamous "Lady in Red," gunned down John Dillinger, famous bank robber and Public Enemy #1, in the alley just south of the theater (just after he watched *Manhattan Melodrama*), thus ensuring the theater a permanent place in local conciousness.

In the following decades, the Biograph Theater slowly declined from a high-class neighborhood theater, to a second-run theater, to third-run theater. By the 1970s, the Biograph was characterized by rows of broken seats, peeling paint, and poor projection. It made a brief comeback as an art house in the 1980s, before closing again in the early 1990s. In the late 1990s, it was bought by the Lowe's chain and converted into a standard multiplex showing first-run films. It was already listed on the National Register of Historic Places when it was designated a Chicago Landmark on March 28, 2001. By that time, however, it had closed again. In 2004, the Victory Gardens Theater purchased the building to stage its own live productions. Architect Daniel P. Coffey constructed a proscenium-thrust stage and restored a grand staircase leading up to the building's second floor. The original marquee was taken down and is now kept at the Chicago History Museum.

THE BIOGRAPH THEATER IS NEAR **DE PAUL University** (Halsted St., Lincoln Ave., and Fullerton Ave.) and the expected congestion of restaurants and sports bars catering to the student and post-graduate crowd. If you want a hint of older Chicago culture, simply take a short walk to two of the city's most popular blues clubs. **Kingston Mines** (2548 N. Halsted St., 773/477-4646), has been Chicago's most famous North Side blues venue since 1968. Visitors have included the Rolling Stones, John (Cougar) Mellencamp, and many other guest jammers. **B.L.U.E.S.** (2519 N. Halsted, 773/528-1012), basically across the street, is a smaller, homier, and friendlier blues club. Both clubs feature live blues seven nights a week.

OLDEST BALLPARK

WRIGLEY FIELD
Clark and Addison streets
(1914)
(Second Oldest in the Country
behind Boston's Fenway Park, 1912)

The ivy, red and white sign, manual scoreboard, neighboring rooftop seats, and the passage of time have turned Wrigley Field into a baseball shrine and museum, visited by people around the world and often sold out. Many Chicagoans remember when Wrigley Field was just a ballpark in a dangerous neighborhood with a bad team and good hot dogs.

On the former site of the Lutheran Theological Seminary, Wrigley Field was built in 1914 at a cost of $250,000. The original ballpark was called Weegham Field and was owned by Charles Weegham, whose team, the Chicago Federals, and later Chicago Whales, played in the Federal League. The team that eventually became the Cubs started playing at the West Side Ballpark in 1885. The first West Side Ball Park was erected in 1885 and located near what are now Congress, Loomis, Harrison, and Throop streets. A newer, larger ballpark was built for the team at Taylor, Wood, and Polk streets in an area now occupied by the University of Illinois Medical Center. In its short life span of just over 20 years, this ballpark was the site of three Cubs pennants, two World Series championships, and the legendary double play combination of Tinkers to Evers to Chance. It also hosted the 1906 World Series between the Chicago Cubs and the Chicago White Sox.

Weegham moved the team to Clark and Addison in 1914. William P. Wrigley bought the Cubs in 1920, and from 1920 to 1926 it was known as Cubs Park. In 1926, the name was changed to Wrigley Field and in 1928 the stadium's seating capacity was increased to 40,000.

Some of the great moments at Wrigley Field include Babe Ruth's famous "called shot," Ernie Banks's 500th home run, and Pete Rose's record-tying 4,191st hit. Aside from a stretch of pennants in the 1930s, the Cubs haven't had much success for the last hundred years. The field held better luck for the Chicago Bears. "The Monsters of the Midway" played at Wrigley Field from 1921 to 1970. During this time, fans saw the great Red Grange and cheered as the team won eight championships on an oddly configured playing field with little room for either a sideline or an end zone.

Wrigley Field has always been a neighborhood ballpark. Longtime Chicagoan Robert Rudd remembers the days when "players like Billy Herman, Bob Rush, and Dizzy and Daffy Dean lived in the Embassy Hotel at Diversey and Pine Grove and used to take the 'L' to the games." During the 1950s, 1960s, and 1970s Wrigley Field still had its small-town charm. Players Rick and Paul Reuschel gave away corn grown on their downstate farms to fans who waited near the players' parking lot after games, and utility infielder Carmen Fanzone would entertain passersby with an occasional trumpet solo.

This all changed in 1984, when the Cubs won their first division title of the new expansion era. The Chicago Tribune Company installed lights in the stadium in 1988. On August eighth of that year, the Cubs played their first night game at Wrigley Field. For many people living around the neighborhood, it seemed like a giant flying saucer had landed at Clark and Addison. At that time, visitors walking through the neighborhood were greeted with the sights of gang graffiti on walls and gym shoes (taken from rival gang members) hanging from the telephone wires. Since then, the area has become a prime example of urban renewal, as the ballpark has brought customers to the bars, restaurants, and nightclubs. Today it stands as a model for a new generation of ballparks, such as Cleveland's Jacob's Field, and is one of Chicago's greatest tourist attractions.

ONCE SCORNED AS AN ANCIENT, OUTDATED relic in the age of AstroTurf and suburban sprawl, Wrigley Field is a now a model ballpark, copied in Cleveland, St. Louis, and dozens of baseball towns throughout the country. The reason—green grass, day baseball, and *Field of Dreams* style baseball purity, right? Wrong! Wrigley Field is an economic powerhouse. Bars, restaurants, and clubs use its proximity to draw free-spending fans and generate millions of dollars for urban centers. "Wrigleyville" has dozens of local hangouts, but the most famous of these is **Murphy's Bleachers** (3653 N. Sheffield Ave., 773/929-7051). Sure, it is a tourist trap. Sure, it is so crowded that after games you can barely lift your elbows. But nestled in the shadows of the famous bleachers, the insanity is part of the Chicago Cubs experience. Another tip: Go there when the Cubs are on the road, or even during the off season. Impeccably managed with excellent, affordable food and some of the finest bartenders in the city, Murphy's is perfect on a warm November day. Step outside for a leisurely walk around the friendly confines, where you can see the statues of Harry Caray and Ernie Banks and commemorative bricks in the sidewalk as well as stand in the shadows of the bleachers and gaze at the rooftop seating vistas and other features so unique to this neighborhood. Then head back into Murphy's and view its own collection of signed Cubs jerseys, photos, and paraphernalia in what is a mini Cubs hall of fame.

OLDEST VERTICAL LIFT BRIDGE

AMTRAK BRIDGE
South Branch of the Chicago River
at Canal Street
(1915)

At the beginning of the twentieth century, Chicago's industrial power was such that the conflict between railroad traffic and merchant ships regularly competed for space along the Chicago River and above it. The solution—a vertical lift bridge. Most Chicagoans are familiar with swing span bridges, which open in two halves through giant pulleys and wheels. If you have ever waited for the sailboats to pass under the Michigan Avenue, State Street, or Dearborn Street bridges, you realize that these bridges are often quite slow. With a vertical lift bridge, the entire bridge is raised and lowered like an elevator.

The giant black iron and cement Amtrak Bridge at Cermak and Canal was built in 1915, and was the heaviest bridge of its kind. One hundred and ninety-five feet high with a main span length of 273 feet and a lifting clearance of 130 feet, it resembles two giant, black iron towers joined by another horizontal bridge. At the top of each tower are giant cement counterweights that are raised and lowered like two ends of a pulley. Resting in the middle of the vertical bar is the bridge tender's station made out of heavily rusted, corrugated steel.

When it was built, the black iron structure perfectly matched the barges and factories blowing out black and gray smoke along the river. Today, it is surrounded by modern warehouses, glass apartment buildings, and the greenery of Chinatown's Ping Tom Park. Still in use by Amtrak trains, it is a reminder of Chicago at the turn of the century and its industrial past.

LOCATED ON THE BANKS OF THE CHICAGO River, the Oldest Vertical Lift Bridge is a short walk west to **Lawrence Fisheries** (2120 S. Canal St., 312/225-2113). A no-nonsense, blue-collar, riverfront fish joint open 24/7, Lawrence Fisheries offers fried perch, catfish, shrimp, and other typical, Chicago-style deep-fried fish. Most seafood items are $7–$10. You can eat inside or outside, but for the nicest option, head east a bit with your food to **Ping Tom Park**. Dedicated to the community of Chinatown, this newer park features a Chinese Garden and riverfront walkway.

OLDEST RELIGIOUS GOODS STORE

ATHENIAN CANDLE
300 S. Halsted Street
(1919)

When we think of Chicago's Greektown, images of packed restaurants with plates of flaming cheese and rotisserie lamb come to mind. But like Chicago's Little Italy (also known simply as Taylor Street), the strip of crowded eateries and bars are primarily tourist-fed remnants of what was once a thriving, ethnic neighborhood.

Athenian Candle Company stands apart as one of the few remaining pieces of Chicago's original Greek immigrant community. Established in 1919, the business still makes its own candles in a little shop in the back. The store also sells a wide variety of incense, crucifixes, novenas, statues, medallions, saints' cards, and other icons of Greek Orthodox, Catholic, and Jewish religious traditions. The first store stood in the midst of Chicago's original Greek neighborhood, known as the Delta. It was on the south side of what is now the Eisenhower Expressway, near the intersection of Polk and Halsted.

"When my father opened his business in 1919, Greektown was located further south," Jean Paspalas, who now manages Athenian Candle, says. "His store was kitty corner to the Hull-House, in what was then a neighborhood of Greeks. We had Greek stores, Greek Orthodox churches, and Greek schools. It was also very crowded, as one building had over 80 Greek families—you can imagine how much fun that was."

Just as it fragmented Taylor Street, the construction of the Eisenhower Expressway and the University of Illinois at Chicago campus hastened the dispersal of this ethnic enclave into the suburbs. "My father came to this location in 1961," Paspalas says. "After that life was never the same. The University of Illinois sent people to the suburbs, or to a smaller Greek area around Lawrence Avenue and Western Avenue. Today, we are the oldest business in Greektown, and besides a pastry shop, a small grocery store, and the music shop, the area is all restaurants. Very few Greek people still live here."

Luckily, Athenian Candle stays put. The business sells religious items alongside things imported from Greece, including the small, finely crafted cups used for serving strong Greek coffee, Greek dolls, and signs that read "Parking for Greeks Only." You can also buy Lucky Dice Soaps, Good Luck and Money Drawing Candles, The Power of the Seven Ancients Incense, and an entire shelf devoted to small vials of strongly scented oils.

"Many of our customers are still Greeks who come from all over the city and the suburbs to purchase the candles, silver icons for the home, and other products that are important parts of the Greek Orthodox religion," Paspalas says. "But in order to survive we have had to become multi-cultural."

Paspalas's son, Themis, now works in the store, marking the third generation of the Paspalas family at Athenian Candle. It is the embodiment of a simple, ethnic, family business, and thus it is important to the culture of Chicago. With its base of regular customers and the thriving popularity of Greektown restaurants drawing curious tourists into the shop as well, it seems that the business will succeed for years to come.

ATHENIAN CANDLE IS LITERALLY AT THE crossroads of Chicago's Greektown. Although it is the oldest business in Greektown, it is certainly not the only one. Known for its Opaaa! (not Oprah, she's a few blocks north and west) flaming cheese, gyros, and festive atmosphere, Chicago's Greektown may have the largest concentration of Greek restaurants outside of Greeece. In the original days of Greektown, restaurants like the Greek Isles were little more than lamb turning on a spit over dirt floors. Now it is a culinary Disneyland. Where to go? Old timers insist that since the **Greek Islands** (200 S. Halsted St., 312/782-9855) owners are "sea people" and the owners of **The Parthenon** (314 S. Halsted St., 312/726-2407) and **Roditys** (222 S. Halsted St., 312/454-0800) are "mountain people," that the Isles is the place for fish and seafood and The Parthenon and Roditys are the places for lamb. But there are many more restaurants than these three "oldest" establishments, which have been around since the late 1960s. Other "newer" restaurants include the charming **Santorini** (800 W. Adams St., 312/829-8820), **Pegasus** (130 S. Halsted St., 312/226-3377), whose rooftop dining comes with a fantastic view of Chicago's West Loop, and **Athena** (212 S. Halsted St., 312/655-0000), with its marvelous outdoor patio.

During the 1970s and 80s, diners could eat until they had to be carted out in a wheelbarrow for as little as ten dollars. The area's surge as a major tourist and business dining spot has meant that prices are a bit higher and portions somewhat smaller, but there is nowhere in the nation, except maybe Detroit, where you can get this variety of lamb, seafood, feta, eggplant, wines, and desserts for your food dollar. Added to this, most establishments have free or valet parking.

But Greektown is more than just restaurants. There is **Greektown Music** (330 S. Halsted St., 312/263-6342), which sells CDs and tapes from Greece; **Byzantium** (232 S. Halsted St., 312/454-1227), a late night bar featuring live, modern-day dance and rock acts from Greece; and **Nine Musses** (315 S. Halsted St., 312/902-9922), which also has late-night partying with a Greek twist. For those with a sweet tooth, **Pan Hellenic Pastries** (322 S. Halsted St., 312/454-1886) offers traditional favorites like baklava and spanikopita in a carryout setting. Tying the neighborhood together is the **Hellenic Museum** (801 W. Adams St., 4th floor, 312/665-1234), home to rotating history and art exhibits, as well as live concerts and other cultural programming.

MARGIE'S CANDIES
1960 N. Western Avenue
(1921)

argie's Candies is a small, street-corner empire that has lasted for almost 90 years. Unlike our landmarks made of steel, glass, and cement, this one is made from chocolate, caramel, ice cream, and fudge.

Margie's Candies has been selling ice cream and candy at the same location since 1921. Greek immigrant Peter George Poulos originally opened it as an ice cream parlor, but it was transformed forever one night in 1933. That was the night Poulos's son sat in a corner booth and proposed to a young girl named Margie Michaels. Over the years, Margie added the trademark handmade truffles, terrapins, toffees, and other candies to the store's vast array of homemade ice cream sundaes, sodas, splits, and shakes. Like the candy, all of the flavorings, ice cream, and foods are homemade. Other than the addition of Margie's delicious creations, not much has changed in the last nine decades.

On the outside, visitors are greeted by a bright red neon sign that simply reads "Margie's Candies" in cursive writing that drips like fudge. Inside, the shop looks like the set of a Shirley Temple movie. Small round tables and traditional ice cream parlor chairs are intertwined with booths done in floral vinyl. Many of the booths feature private Seeburg jukeboxes (the forerunner of the iPod) topped off with stained glass and etched mirrors. The shop is lined with wooden shelving crowded with memorabilia, including clay containers for Thompson's Malted Milk Balls, stainless steel milk jugs, and china and Kewpee dolls. The crown jewel of Margie's Candies is a glass display case filled with Beatles memorabilia, including albums, posters, and a signed photo from the night in 1964 when the Fab Four snacked at the shop after a Comiskey Park concert. Also in the case is a picture of Al Capone, a not-so-sweet guy who nevertheless indulged his sweet tooth at Margie's Candies.

Of course, the main attraction at Margie's Candies is not the décor but the ice cream, which is 18 percent butter fat. Some of the store's creations include the Eiffel Tower (four scoops of ice cream, bananas, and topping piled high and narrow), the Coco-Loco Sundae (coconut ice cream and chocolate syrup), the Brownie Ala Mode, the Zombie, the Fudge Atomic Sundae, and the World's Largest Sundae (over half a gallon of ice cream). Other treats include sodas, malts, pies, cheesecakes, phosphates, and egg creams. Oh, and sandwiches and salads.

The restaurant is still owned by Peter and Christina Poulos, the original owner's grandchildren, who acknowledge that their restaurant has been built not only out of ice cream and candy, but a lot of love. "If I had a penny for everybody who was engaged here," Poulos laughs, "I would be a millionaire."

BACK IN THE DAY, WHILE TWO TEENAGERS or well-meaning adults were holding hands, eating sundaes, and sipping sodas at Margie's, there was another, more sinister brand of entertainment going on in Bucktown. Remnants of that survive today at **Lottie's Pub** (1925 W. Cortland St., 773/489-0738), now mainly a sports bar, with burgers, nachos, salads, darts, and games for a new generation of bar-goers. *But oh, if the walls could talk!* Opened in 1934 by Walter "Lottie" Zagorski, "Zagorski's," and later "Lottie's," were alleged dens of vice. According to old-timers, the bar, especially its basement ("Zagorski's Rathskeller"), offered gambling, strip tease parties, all-night poker games, mingling with mobsters, and more. Standing six-foot tall and able to toss out unruly patrons with a single hand, Zagorski was a transvestite, and an old photograph that still hangs in the bar does reveal a person in a flowered dress with a high forehead, square jaw, and wide, broad shoulders. Another vintage bar in Bucktown is the **Lincoln Tavern** (1858 W. Wabansia Ave., 773/342-7778). A Prohibition-era ice cream parlor and apartment turned into a bar after the dreaded law was repealed, it is now run by the Folak family. With wooden paneling, a cozy feel, and some of the best roast duck in the city, the Lincoln Tavern is a neighborhood joint that has remained largely unchanged since the neighborhood's blue-collar days.

OLDEST BOWLING ALLEY

 SOUTHPORT LANES
3325 N. Southport Avenue
(1922)

Southport Lanes is Chicago's oldest bowling alley and the only bowling alley to still employ pin boys to remove and re-set bowling pins after each roll. During the last century, however, the building at 3325 North Southport has also housed a tavern, pool hall, gambling den, restaurant, and brothel—a veritable one-stop shopping spot for West Lake View residents interested in amusement and sin.

"The building was built in the early 1900s by Schlitz as a place where they could both sell beer and house their draft horses for the neighborhood," Steve Sobele, the current owner of Southport Lanes explains. "Like Schubas down the street, it was built as a 'tied house' with the giant terra cotta globe and Schlitz logo adorning the side of the building."

During the late nineteenth and early twentieth centuries, tied houses sprung up throughout Chicago. The City of Chicago tried to reduce the number of crime-ridden taverns by raising the price for a liquor license to a rate that many small bar owners could no longer afford. The breweries, which included Atlas, Blatz, Pabst, Miller, Peter Hand, and Birk Brothers, as well as Schlitz, saw an opening. They paid the licensing fee and erected taverns. In exchange, bar owners were obliged to sell only the beer produced by the sponsoring brewery. Soon major breweries were not only in the business of making beer, but distributing and selling it as well. New laws prohibited these monopolies, and the outrage over the power of the major breweries helped fuel efforts to enact the Prohibition Laws of 1919.

At the start of 1922, the building at 3325 North Southport was a tavern known as "The Nook" but soon both the physical layout and use of the building drastically changed. "In 1922 the business was suffering from Prohibition, so the large bar that used to be on the south wall was moved and replaced with the bowling lanes," Sobele says. "A smaller bar was built on the north wall, but when we took over in 1991, the former owner, Leo Beitz, told me more about the building's history. Apparently there was a house of ill repute on the second floor. There was even a dumbwaiter that was used to carry food and drinks upstairs, and if you look where the shoe rack is you can still see remnants of it."

The original murals above the bar and the bowling lanes show nymph-like women dressed in flowing white gowns, beckoning like the sirens of Ulysses. The rest of the establishment features many other restored elements of the original building, most notably the pressed tin ceilings over the billiards room.

At the end of Prohibition in 1933 the building was again used as a full service bar and bowling alley. "The building continued as a bowling alley, but in the 1940s another wing was added on just to the east," Sobele explains. "According to Beitz, the building's usage went from prostitution to gambling. This made sense as when we were remodeling the building in the 1990s we saw trunks filled with bundles of wires. Apparently, these were phone or telegraph lines which went directly to the racetracks around the country. It was a set up right out of the movie *The Sting*."

In the 1950s Beitz took over, and turned the building into a more tame combination of bowling alley and beer hall downstairs, with rooms for rent upstairs. Sobele bought the building and the business in 1991.

At that time, the bowling alley still used live pinsetters to clear and re-set the bowling pins, a job that had almost universally given way to automation. "I remember when we bought the building, I said to myself, 'I'd hate to be the guy who has to fire all the pin boys,' so I didn't," Sobele says. "As time went on I began to like the historical aspects of it, and now there is a certain nostalgia to the fact that we are the last place in Chicago to still use live pin boys."

Sitting in a cockpit that runs about waist high, the pin boys must kneel, stoop, bend over to get pins and bowling balls, and stack pins. This is done with echo of balls rolling, pins crashing, and music and conversation blaring, all amplified down the corridors of the bowling lanes. "Most of the people who work as pin boys are high school guys or people who work in the kitchen who want a change of pace," Sobele shares. "Lately it has been getting harder to find people who want to do it." The job pays minimum wage, but the big benefit of the gig is the tips. Regular customers, on the last ball of the last game, fill the holes in the bowling balls with bills and send them down the alley.

Sobele sees no reason to change this policy, or the century-old building that houses his business. Since Sobele bought it in 1991, Southport Lanes has risen with the explosion of businesses along Southport Avenue. The notorious brothel upstairs was converted to rooms for rent and then offices. This nightspot honors the tradition of fun and amusement at 3325 North Southport, as it not only offers three bowling lanes, six pool tables and a full menu, but also 16 draft beers, 43 bottled beers, and 23 different varieties of Scotch whiskey.

MAYEUR

SOUTHPORT LANES IS LOCATED IN WHAT was once a run-down neighborhood and is now the hub of west Wrigleyville's dining, shopping, and nightlife. We already mentioned **Schubas Tavern** (3159 N. Southport Ave., 773/525-2508), another "tied house" that has nightly live music. Also close to Southport Lanes is the **Music Box Theatre** (see Oldest Movie Theater, p. 171) and **Wrigley Field** (see Oldest Ballpark, p. 123), six blocks northeast.

OLDEST BREAKFAST RESTAURANT

LOU MITCHELL'S
565 W. Jackson Boulevard
(1923)

"I hate this time of year, just after Christmas, until the end of February," Heleen Thanos, manager of Lou Mitchell's, says. "Business is so slow!" It is ten o'clock on a snowy January morning, and temperatures are struggling to make it out of the single digits. Inside Lou Mitchell's, however, the smell of bacon, pancake syrup, and freshly brewed coffee is tantalizing patrons who, even after the breakfast rush, wait in line for a table.

While most restaurants would love to have more customers than tables at off-hours, Lou Mitchell's often has customers lined up out the door and down Jackson Boulevard waiting to get in. A Chicago institution, regular customers at Lou Mitchell's include lawyers, stockbrokers, commodity traders, office workers, and tradesmen. Its list of patrons includes politicians such as President George W. Bush, President Jimmy Carter, and Mayor Richard M. Daley, and celebrities like Nicolas Cage, Dennis Rodman, and Muhammad Ali. All pile in for the restaurant's specialty: hearty breakfasts of eggs, potatoes, pancakes, and bacon or sausage, served in thick, stainless steel skillets. After over 85 years in business, Lou Mitchell's has not changed its formula for success.

"The restaurant opened in 1923 as a diner by William Mitchell, who called it 'Mitchell's Cupboard,'" Thanos says. "At that time this area was the garment district, and you also had a lot of printers who worked in Printers Row a few blocks away. We are also close to Union Station, and before it moved, the Greyhound Bus Terminal was also near here."

If pressmen, tailors, and hungry travelers from around the country were not enough to fill the diner's swivel seats and long counters, changes in the nation's transportation system provided even greater opportunities, as Route 66 officially began about a quarter mile east. "In 1926, they opened Route 66, so we began to get hungry truck drivers coming in for breakfast before or after a long haul on the road," Thanos relates.

This bounty of customers and Lou Mitchell's menu of hearty, inexpensive breakfast food was enough to keep the restaurant going through the Great Depression.

"The original owner, William Mitchell, passed away in 1943, so his son, Lou took over and changed the name to what it is now, Lou Mitchell's," Thanos says. "The place also expanded in the 1940s. It used to be just a little breakfast and lunch counter, but they added booths, more tables, and waitresses."

Business boomed with the baby boomers through the 1950s and 1960s. During the 1970s and 1980s, the Loop experienced a downturn as people moved to the suburbs. Travelers who used to arrive by train at Union Station started to take airplanes in-

stead. But the restaurant didn't seem to miss a beat. Notices
from visiting presidents and dignitaries didn't hurt business, and
neither did the publicity gained from the filming of movies at
the restaurant like *The Untouchables*.

After 70 years in the Mitchell family, the restaurant changed
hands in 1993. "In 1984 'Uncle Lou' retired, and his nephew Nick
took over the business. Then in 1992, he put it up for sale," Thanos says. "A lot of people wanted to buy it. My grandfather and
uncle, who came from Greece, had a diner at Van Buren and
Wacker. The owner had no children, so they figured, with us
being Greeks and all, they would keep it in 'the family,' so to
speak."

The Thanos family sustained the many traditions that have
given Lou Mitchell's the title of oldest breakfast restaurant in
Chicago. One thing that brings customers back is "The World's
Finest Coffee," a special blend of Superior Coffee that is produced in Chicago. Another trait is that each customer receives
a small box of Milk Duds upon entering the restaurant. "Back
in those days, there weren't as many candy bars as you have
today," Thanos reminds me. "You had Baby Ruth, Butterfinger,
Hershey's. During the 1950s, the owner of the company Leaf
Co. had his office on Ontario and Franklin, and he used to come
in all the time. He kept telling us about this new candy, Milk
Duds, and he wanted Lou to buy the candy and sell it in the
store. Lou figured he wouldn't buy it and sell it, but buy it and
give it away." Such features give Lou Mitchell's its special place
in Chicago lore. It is so special, in fact, that in May 2006 the Illinois Historic Preservation Agency made Lou Mitchell's a state
landmark.

As the customers file in on a cold January morning, few are
concerned about the restaurant's historic status. All they want
is hot cup of coffee and generous portions of omelets and pancakes. "Lou Mitchell's is the oldest restaurant in the city...it is

old-world Americana," Thanos says. "We are unique in that while everything downtown keeps changing, we are here. A lot of our staff has been here for 10 or 20 years, so when a customer comes in he or she not only sees a familiar building, menu, and booth, but a familiar face that offers old-time, personal hospitality and service as well."

☞ ONCE, LOU MITCHELL'S WAS IN THE CENTER of Chicago's printing district and along the famous Route 66. Alas, no longer, but it is still a hop, skip, and a jump (about one block west) of Chicago's **Union Station** (Canal St. between Adams St. and Jackson Blvd., www.chicagounionstation. com). Completed in 1925, it comes to us from America's classic era of massive railroad stations. And massive it is, as the building has 20,000 square feet of terra cotta, Corinthian columns, and pink Tennessee marble. This period grandeur made it the right setting for filming scenes for Brian De Palma's *The Untouchables* (1987). The station saw as many as 100,000 passengers a day during the World War II era. It also had its own police force, jail, and infirmary. Although railroad traffic has declined, several Amtrak trains such as the Empire Builder, California Zephyr, and City of New Orleans still run through the station, and these, along with the Metra commuter trains, keep Union Station buzzing.

OLDEST CHILI PARLOR

 LINDY'S CHILI
3685 S. Archer Avenue
(1924)

There has always been some dispute as to whether chili was invented in Mexico or in Texas. Research conducted by a new generation of Tex-Mex chefs has proven that chili was indeed the concoction of cowboy cooks on Texas cattle drives. Combining dried beans, chilis, garlic, onions, and beef (or whatever else was skinned that afternoon) offered a cheap, mobile, and tasty way to feed cowboys.

Chili was first introduced to Chicago when a restaurant from Texas set up a San Antonio chili stand at the 1893 Columbian Exposition. But the dish really caught on in the northern states when a new kind of roving cowboy, the truck driver, hit the highways looking for an inexpensive, portable way to eat on the move. Lindy's Chili's longtime link with the 18-wheeler is evident the first time you walk through the door. Looking out the window down Archer Avenue near Western and Pershing, and just off the Stevenson and Dan Ryan expressways, you can't go more than 20 seconds without seeing some kind of truck go by. When Lindy's Chili first opened in 1924, the Brighton Park area was surrounded by truck yards, but also by two rail lines, several factories, and the stockyards.

Today, a 25´ x 20´ black and white photograph of Lindy's circa the 1930s hangs over the counter with a caption proudly reading, "Lindy's, Chicago's Oldest Chili Parlor." The picture shows bartenders wearing white aprons. Behind them is a full bar featuring assorted whiskeys and spirits and a neon sign advertising Fox De Luxe, a beer that was once the pride of the South Side. Today, there are still taps for Miller and other brands of beer.

The business has joined up with another South Side favorite, Gertie's Ice Cream, established at 55th Street and California Avenue in 1901. In the late 1960s, the prevalence of ice cream in grocery stores and an abundance of new franchises such as Baskin-Robbins spelled hard times for Gertie's. A neighborhood resident and longtime customer, John Yesutis, purchased Lindy's Chili, and his brother purchased Gertie's Ice Cream; the two men then combined the businesses. "Lindy's was drawing huge lunch and dinner crowds, but slowed in the evenings. On the other hand, Gertie's Ice Cream did great business in the evenings when customers crowded in," Yesutis says. "Additionally, there were seasonal factors that affected business. Cold Chicago winters bolstered chili sales, while ice cream sales declined. And, of course, in the summer, ice cream soared past chili sales."

Giant ice cream dishes now stand alongside the beer glasses and taps. A dining room has also been added behind the original counter. Other than that, little has changed at Lindy's. At lunchtime, men in work boots with their names stitched on oval patches saunter in through the door for a steaming bowl of chili.

The chili is offered over macaroni (a.k.a. chili mac) with cavatelli noodles, over spaghetti, on burgers, on hot dogs, and—every waistline's favorite—as chili cheese fries. Lindy's also serves Filbert's Root Beer (see Oldest Soda Pop Maker, p. 154), burgers, beer, sundaes, splits, and phosphate fountain drinks.

The merger between two neighborhood favorites has been so successful that Lindy's has become a local franchise. Today, you can get chili, beer, and ice cream at the original location at 3685 South Archer Avenue, but also at 76th and Pulaski, 111th and Kedzie, and 6544 South Archer Avenue in Chicago. You can also visit Lindy's in the suburbs at 87th and Harlem in Bridgeview, 2353 South Laramie Avenue in Cicero, 3000 West Jefferson Street in Joliet, 15501 South Cicero Avenue in Oak Forest, and 100 Commercial Drive in Morris.

☞ LINDY'S CHILI IS A HUB OF THE SOUTHWEST Side's Brighton Park neighborhood. Another focal point is **McKinley Park** (Bounded by Western Ave., 37th St., Damen Ave., and Pershing Rd.). Located just south of Lindy's, it was once the site of cabbage patches and the Brighton Park Racetrack (built in 1855 by Mayor "Long" John Wentworth). Planned in 1902, shortly after the assassination of President McKinley, it features ball fields, tennis courts, walking areas, and the McKinley Park lagoon. Back then, this grassy area was an oasis for both the workers and the neighbors of Chicago's Union Stock Yards, which were about one-half mile east. The lagoon is the jewel of McKinley Park. Once used as a swimming area, it's is now the home of hundreds of geese, as well as bluegill, carp, and other pond/sport fish. The lagoon is also famous for being the spot where the first Asian Carp, a giant, invading species that threatens the entire waterway system, was caught in the Chicago area.

OLDEST CHINESE RESTAURANT OLDEST NEON SIGN

ORANGE GARDEN RESTAURANT
1942 W. Irving Park Road
(1924)

Orange Garden Restaurant has been around since 1925. (This makes it just slightly older than Chinatown's oldest operating restaurant, Wan Kow, which opened in 1927 at 2237 South Wentworth Avenue.) At that time, most of the city's Chinese population lived near Wentworth and 22nd Street (now Cermak Road) in Chicago's booming Chinatown neighborhood.

Chinese immigrants began arriving in Chicago in the late 1800s, and the city's first documented Chinese resident was a character with the moniker of Opium Dong, who owned a store on South Clark Street. By 1905, most of the Chinese residents settled around Harrison Street and Wabash Avenue, in the South Loop area now occupied by the campuses of Roosevelt University and Columbia College. The Chinese Americans maintained a close association with the warlords who ran China. In Chicago, the Hip Sing Tong controlled the original Chinatown, at Harrison and Clark. However, in February of 1912, the On Leongs took over much of mainland China. The immigrants' ties to their native land were so deep and the hold of the warlords so strong that even a continent away the Chinese community moved en masse from the Hip Sing territory to what is now considered "Chinatown": 22nd Street and Wentworth Avenue, which was controlled by the On Leongs.

In 1926, Orange Garden's first owner, a man named W. Chan, opened the restaurant in what was then the city's far North Side. He was immediately presented with a predicament. How do you sell exotic Chinese food to Americans? One way was to offer Americanized dishes like chop suey, chow mien, and fried egg rolls. The other was to make Orange Garden look American. Chan accomplished that with decorating the interior with black leather booths, stainless steel lights fixtures, Chinese lacquer pictures, and paper lanterns, and by surrounding the outside with Art Deco stainless steel and lighting it up with neon. The orange and green sign that reads "Orange Garden, Chop Suey, Chow Mein" is the oldest neon sign in Chicago. This sign does not feature the blinking, dancing lights and bold colors of many of Chicago's great neon signs of the past. Instead, its subdued, consistent glow, combined with an orange and blue neon sign that reads "Chop Suey to Take Home," stainless steel borders, and wide windows, transform the Orange Garden from an "exotic" Chinese restaurant to a familiar diner.

Inside, the restaurant has barely changed since it opened over 85 years ago. The waitstaff still wear white shirts with black bowties. The food is take-out or eat-in American Cantonese: fried rice, won ton soup, egg rolls, and chow mein. When you eat at Orange Garden, though, you are getting far more than your average strip mall food. If you sit inside long enough, you might hear Benny Goodman on the radio or see a trolley car rumble down Irving Park Road. How many times have you walked or driven down Irving and seen Orange Garden and its neon signage? These places—small, almost hidden, establishments—should be recognized as an active part of Chicago's history.

ORANGE GARDEN HAS WITNESSED THE neighborhood around it change many times. The North Center area has over the past 30 years gone from solid working-class to clearly gentrified. It's overwhelmingly residential, but with some standout establishments near its main Irving Park Road-Lincoln Avenue-Damen Avenue intersection. **Katerina's** (1920 W. Irving Park Rd., 773/ 348-7592) is a jazz club that specializes in vocalists and soft guitar music while eschewing be-bop. **Resi's Bierstube** (2034 W. Irving Park Rd., 773/472-1749), one of the last remaining German restaurants in the city, is beloved for its amazing summertime beer garden (the city's oldest) out back. It's been a bar at least as far back as 1913, but has been Resi's since 1965. For some of the best breakfasts (and regular evening banjo music, comedy, and offbeat lectures), there's the veteran **Lincoln Restaurant** (4008 N. Lincoln Ave., 773/248-1820), whose menu has omelets named after Civil War generals and ice cream sundaes named after American presidents.

agician Ben Whiting is standing behind the counter at Magic Inc., holding a deck of cards. "Pick a card," he says, citing the classic line. I stick my hand out and lift a four of clubs from the deck.

"This is your card," he says questioning me. "Are you sure?" I nod. "Well, just to make sure, sign the card, then place your hand over it."

I sign the card with a bright red marker and guard it with my right hand. In the meantime, Whiting begins blowing up a small purple balloon.

"Don't watch the balloon," he reminds. "Keep guarding the card."

He blows up the balloon and shakes it. "Do you hear something?"

I shake the balloon. Yes, it's rattling. Whiting hands me a pocket knife and I pop the balloon.

"What is this," he says as he opens the balloon. I look and it is my signed four of clubs, folded into pieces, which has somehow escaped from under my hand and hidden inside of the balloon. I lift my hand and the card is gone. Welcome to the world of Magic Inc.

"We have been here since 1926, and are the oldest family-run magic shop in North America," says owner Sandy Marshall, who is a magician, two-time Emmy Award-winning TV screenwriter, and New York playwright. "That was the year Houdini died. My father Jay Marshall, the company's originator, saw him when he was seven years old. On that night Houdini walked through a wall."

Inspired, Jay Marshall went on to a career as a magician. Some of his many accomplishments include eighteen appearances on the Ed Sullivan Show, brandishing his magic in the Ziegfeld Follies and three Broadway shows, opening for Frank Sinatra, and being voted as Dean of the Society of American Magicians. Sandy Marshall's mother was Francis Ireland, an accomplished magician who specialized in children's magic; her father (Sandy's grandfather) was also a Dean of the Society of American Magicians.

"There have only been eight Deans of the Society of American Magicians, and two of them were my father and grandfather," Marshall says. "So I have about one quarter of the Society's history in my veins."

Along the way, Francis Ireland and Jay Marshall also opened Magic Inc.

"We were originally located west of the Loop on Halsted, and then moved to 109 North Dearborn. In 1963 we moved here," Sandy Marshall reports.

The shop is filled not only with magic dice, cards, cups, wands, books on magic, and colorful magicians' costumes, but also with posters and advertisements for famous magicians active throughout the shop's tenure.

"The first half of the twentieth century was the Golden Age of Magic," Marshall says. "You had Houdini in the 1920s, and then greats like Thurston and Blackstone, as well as his son Harry Blackstone Jr. It was, in many ways, a simpler time. I mean, having a girl vanish behind a truck is still impressive, but we have to compete against all the special effects from movies and the internet now."

Besides being a store where young magicians can hang out, purchase tricks, and learn their craft, Magic Inc. is also the headquarters for many local magicians. At the time of the interview, the legendary magician Cellini had suffered a stroke. Marshall, Whiting, and the rest of the staff were busy assembling other great magicians like Marshall Brodien (Bozo's Wizzo the Wizard, TV Magic Cards), Thomas Medina (The Amazing Thomas), and Benjamin Barnes to perform at a benefit to be held in the shop's backroom theater.

"At one time we had 18 magicians working here," Marshall says. "I had to come here from New York because our last manager decided that this place should be all business and no fun, and business started to fail. Magic is fun and magicians are mostly adults who never grow up," Marshall says. "So if you have magic without fun, you don't have magic."

LOCATED NEAR THE CORNER OF FOSTER and Lincoln, Magic Inc. is about one-half mile west of Chicago's old Swedish settlement and current center for bars, culture, and restaurants: the Andersonville neighborhood. At the turn of the twentieth century, Swedes, Norwegians, and other Northern Europeans flocked to the area, a lineage evident in the name of the local high school, **Roald Amundsen**, at Foster and Damen avenues. Other Scandinavian holdovers include the **Swedish-American Museum** (5211 N. Clark, 773/728-8111), where you can see traditional Swedish costumes, clogs, and other arts and crafts. The museum is open 10 AM–4 PM Tuesday through Friday; 11 AM–4 PM Saturday and Sunday. If you are interested in food, **Ann Sather** (5207 N. Clark, 773/271-6677) offers Swedish meatballs, crepes, and hot cinnamon rolls to die for, 7 AM–2 PM during the week; 7 AM–4 PM weekends. Other Andersonville hot spots include the **Hop Leaf** (5148 N. Clark, 773/334-9851), offering the best selection of Belgian beers in the city, with over 20 on tap and at least 30 in bottles. **Reza's Restaurant**, another local standby, opened back in the day when hummus was still "exotic." It's now a Middle Eastern emporium, open from 11 AM–midnight seven days a week, with the lamb shank and the broiled catfish being of special interest. Finally, if you are into the true Swedish drinking experience, you must sample the glogg or Mallort at **Simon's Tavern** (5210 N. Clark, 773/878-0894). Rumored to take the glue off of wallpaper, a serious drink for serious drinkers, Mallort is a local product with a cult following on Chicago's North Side.

OLDEST SODA POP MAKER

{ **FILBERT'S**
3430 S. Ashland Avenue
(1926) }

When you walk into Filbert's Root Beer, the first thing you hear is the clinking of the clear glass bottles being hand packed into crates. Yes, clear glass bottles, and yes, hand packed. A local product since 1926, Filbert's is truly a mom-and-pop soda pop company. Located in a single small warehouse on the near South Side, Filbert's is the last of Chicago's family-owned soda pop makers. In the days before Coke and Pepsi, mass production, distribution, and refrigeration, almost every neighborhood had its own local soda pop maker. Just like draft beer, soda pop was made and distributed daily, delivered every morning throughout the neighborhood.

"My great grandfather, George Filbert began by delivering coal, milk, and ice to Bridgeport families in the early 1900s,"

Ronald George Filbert Jr., who owns the company today, says. "Then in 1926, his son George Filbert began to make root beer."

This decision sparked the golden age of Filbert's Root Beer. Although Prohibition did not stop neighborhood brewers like Fox De Luxe and Canadian Ace from producing beer and "needle beer" (non-alcoholic beer later injected with alcohol by syringe so inspectors could not spot tampering on the barrels), the company did see a marked spike in their root beer sales. "Back then it was made in half barrels, and we supplied root beer to taverns in five states," Filbert says.

Filbert's no longer makes their root beer in barrels, but you can still taste the radical difference between their sarsaparilla and the mass-produced product. Even Dad's Root Beer, which had a major bottling plant in Chicago, is made with so much carbonation and consumed at such cold temperatures that the flavor is of acidic bubbles tinged with root beer. Filbert's actually tastes like root beer!

The company produces a complete line of soda pops. Once again, Filbert's differs from their corporate rivals by offering over 18 flavors, including watermelon, cream soda, grapefruit, blue raspberry, peach, and pineapple.

Like Chicago's alcoholic breweries and other neighborhood soda pop makers (such as Lasser's on the North Side), Filbert's also saw their market share shrink to almost nothing after World War II. Unlike beer makers, Filbert's hung on by mainly selling to Bridgeport restaurants, ice cream parlors, and small stores. Coke and Pepsi probably sell more soda pop in a minute than Filbert's does in a year, but does bigger always mean better?

SOME SAY THAT WHEN PUBLIC (OR CITY) sponsorship of a venue fails, that private industry will take over. This happened with the closing of the original Maxwell Street market on the Near West Side spawning the "new Maxwell Street market" in the South Loop, as well as several imitators around the city. One of these is Bridgeport's **Swap-O-Rama** (4100 S. Ashland Ave., 773/376-6993). A private outdoor flea market held in a series of giant parking lots (there are indoor vendors, too) three blocks west of Filbert's, shoppers can find a lot of what was at the old Maxwell Street market at Swap-O-Rama—tools, CDs, light furniture, clothing, electronics, car parts, bootlegs, knock-offs, hot merchandise, and more. Old-time merchants, however, say it is a far cry from the real thing (consider the indoor restrooms and snack bars). Open weekends. There is a $1 admission charge.

OLDEST ITALIAN RESTAURANT

 ITALIAN VILLAGE
71 W. Monroe Street
(1927)

When you think of a third-generation, mom-and-pop business, you usually think of a neighborhood. Italian Village is a third-generation, old-values business, but its neighborhood is the lights, sights, and hustle and bustle of the center of the Loop.

When you walk into Italian Village, its intimate booths, glowing "starlit" ceiling, piano bar, tropical fish tanks, ornate murals, and Italianate décor transport you to another world. Unlike the new theme restaurants that line their walls with faux old Italian wine barrels, olive oil bottles, and paintings, at Italian Village the candid photos of stars like Barbra Streisand, Frank and Nancy Sinatra, and Julie Andrews tell you that it is the real thing.

A short walk east from the First National and other La Salle Street banks and a few blocks southwest of Marshall Field's
(now Macy's), Italian Village is surrounded by history. When
the restaurant opened in 1927, it was next door to the old Monroe Theater, one of the first buildings designed for motion pictures, and the site of the famed *Inter Ocean* newspaper, which
employed writers like Ring Lardner. Sure, the location has
helped Italian Village has survive for over 75 years, but just think
of how many other establishments have come and gone in that
same period!

"The reasons why we have survived so long are simple," Alfredo Capitanini, grandson of the original owner, says. "We
serve good food at reasonable prices, and the customer is always
right. I mean, we have three restaurants here within one building so if somebody wants say, duck, at one in the morning, we'll
search all of our kitchens until we find it."

Italian Village consists of three restaurants: the original
Village, La Cantina, and Vivre. The Village serves traditional
Southern Italian family-style fare such as pasta and red sauce,
eggplant parmesan, and veal and chicken dishes. La Cantina
is an Italian-style steak and seafood house. Vivere is a modern
trattoria-type establishment that offers wild game such as rabbit
and pheasant, as well as squid and other dishes that were more
traditionally the diet of Italy's thriving merchant class. The two-
and-a-half story building also has a wine cellar holding 40,000
bottles. As you can imagine, it did not all begin this way.

Sitting in a cozy, semi-private booth that is one of the signature nooks and crannies of Italian Village, Capitanini talked
history. "My father Alfredo came here from Tuscany in 1924. He
started working as a dishwasher at a restaurant called The Florence, and as soon as his shift was over, he went over to work as
a cook at a place called The Garden of Italy, which was on Randolph Street. He and a partner were able to start what would

eventually become the Italian Village in 1927." Capitanini says, "At that time, there were 75 restaurants in the Loop. You had new movie palaces, the opera, everybody shopped at Marshall Field's or Carson's, and the people who attended the shows, operas, or symphonies always dined out. I mean, it was the Roaring Twenties."

A short time later, the stock market crashed and the Great Depression hit. The senior Capitanini had to resort to money-saving measures like growing tomatoes, herbs, and vegetables in his expansive home garden, which is still in use today. As the owner of a new restaurant, he had to think quickly to bring in customers. It was at this time that Capitanini incorporated many of the features that distinguished Italian Village and made it a local favorite. These features include the enclosed booths that seat up to ten guests. They are named *La Prigione* (the jail), *Il Convento* (the convent), *Casa Reale* (the king's palace), *La Posta* (the post office) *La Taverna* (the tavern), *La Banca* (the bank), and *La Pergola* (the gazebo). To make the restaurant even more inviting to children and romantic to adults, Capitanini had white and colored lights inserted into the dark sky blue ceiling so diners could imagine they were sitting under an Italian sky.

In a city that had previously known only Southern Italian dishes, Capitanini introduced specialties from other regions and invented dishes of his own. In 1931, he introduced cannelloni and manicotti to Chicagoland, and added dishes like fettucini alfredo, saltimbocca ala romano, and others to the menu. "We have been serving pizza for over 60 years," Capitanini says. "In fact, we are sitting in a room that was once the little kitchen where a lady used to make pizzas. My grandfather also came up with the first Chicken Vesuvio."

After Capitanini endured the Great Depression, he was rewarded with the post-war boom of the late 1940s and early 1950s. Not only was this an apex of American prosperity, it was also a time when Americans fell in love with Italian-American culture. Like sushi is (or was), pizza became a favorite food of suburban America. Spaghetti, once eaten only by immigrants, became a fixture of the average American diet. On the cultural front, Italian stars like Frank Sinatra, Sophia Loren, and Dean Martin ("when the moon hits your eye like a big pizza pie, that's amore") populated the hit parade and the silver screen. The restaurant expanded, and Capitanini looked to his family for more help.

"My Aunt Ave, Uncle Ray, and my father Frank become the second generation to run the Italian Village in 1955," Capitanini says. "It was about this time that they opened the second restaurant, La Cantina, in the basement. In 1961 my uncle Ray opened the Florentine Room, which some say was the first gourmet Italian restaurant in Chicago." At that time restaurants like the Pump Room, Don Roth's Blackhawk Restaurant, and other lavish eateries offered fine food, fancy décor, and entertainment. But the Florentine Room held its own and a short time later it was named Chicago's best Italian restaurant by the *Chicago Tribune.*

Like the Pump Room, Italian Village and the Florentine Room, local celebrities in their own right, have attracted generations of star performers. "Many people from the world of opera, including Placido Domingo, Luciano Pavarotti, and Maria Callas have come here," Capitanini says. "More importantly, the Lyric Opera's Bruno Bartoletti, and former artistic directors Carol Fox, Ardis Krainik, and many others made this a regular place to meet after performances." While many local restaurants display signed pictures of local politicians and TV newscasters on their walls, Italian Village's walls display a collage of national, household-name celebrities from many eras. These include Barbra Streisand, Faye Dunaway, playwright and composer Moss Hart (of the Rodgers and Hart team), and Saul Bellow, just to name a few.

The 1970s brought a bit of a downturn for Italian Village. "If you last this long, you have to survive what can often be a roller coaster of good and bad years," Capitanini says. "The 1970s saw the closing of a lot of the large movie theaters like the Oriental, the United Artists, and the Woods, and the theater business also dropped off. State Street died down, and most of the places south of the river had a hard time."

The 1990s ushered in a dining fashion towards chicken, fish, and lighter fare. At the same time, Al and Gina Capitanini became the third generation from the Capitanini family to run Italian Village. Long running shows like *Les Misérables*, *The Phantom of the Opera*, and *Wicked* brought people back to the large newly renovated downtown theaters. While the demand for Italian food has risen, so too have the supply of restaurants. "Right now we are battling against competition from the newer Northern style Italian restaurants on the North Side and chains, like Rosebud, Tuscany, and Maggiano's," Capitanini says. "But we will survive because I think we are more than a restaurant. We are a destination."

ITALIAN VILLAGE HAS STAYED OPEN SINCE 1926, in part due to its proximity to Macy's (111 N. State St.), formerly **Marshall Field's** (the iconic clock at State & Washington streets is still there); the **Civic Opera House** (20 N. Wacker Dr.); and the Louis Sullivan building that formerly housed **Carson Pirie Scott** (1 S. State St.). In their day—even recently!—they were popular destinations. Today, they are architectural landmarks. You can hunt for these landmarks one by one, but the Italian Village is also about one-quarter mile from the **Chicago Architecture Foundation** (224 S. Michigan Ave., 312/922-3432), an architecture educational and advocacy organization that conducts tours by bus, boat, Segway, train, bicycle, and foot. A dizzying lineup of tours includes historic skyscrapers, Tiffany treasures, sculptures in the Loop, a Chicago River cruise, Frank Lloyd Wright in Oak Park, and many more. They also have permanent and changing exhibitions, a book/gift shop, free lunchtime lectures, special evening events, and youth programs like the Newhouse High School Architecture Competition. And yes, a meal and a glass of wine at Italian Village, a landmark in its own right, would be a great way to end a day of enjoying Chicago's world-class architecture.

OLDEST INDOOR, OLYMPIC-SIZED (NOW JUNIOR OLYMPIC) SWIMMING POOL

THE MEDINAH ATHLETIC CLUB
(now Hotel InterContinental)
505 N. Michigan Avenue
(1929)

The Medinah Temple Natatorium is more than a pool. Featuring terra cotta fountains, balconies, and thousands of hand-laid tiles surrounding an Olympic (now Junior Olympic) pool, it is a 1920s fantasy straight out of Hollywood's Coconut Grove or a Rudolph Valentino movie. It historically has been a hangout for actors, writers, and celebrities, from former Olympian and *Tarzan* star Johnny Weissmuller to swimming-pool–movie goddess Esther Williams.

The pool attracted stars and celebrities even after the athletic club became a hotel in the 1940s. I worked first as a lifeguard and then manager of the health facility from 1981 to 1986, when it was the Radisson Hotel. During this time, celebrities, including Sugar Ray Leonard, 1960s icon Donovan, Chicago's reigning mystery queen novelist Sara Paretsky, and an aging Tennessee Williams, sought refuge in the pool's aqua blue waters.

In its Jazz-age heyday, the Medinah Athletic Club featured a gym, running track, bowling alley, golf range, boxing area, archery range, and two shooting galleries! Designed by architect Walter Ahlschlager, the athletic club was part of the Medinah Temple complex located at 505 North Michigan Avenue, which also held Assyrian-style ballrooms, guest rooms, banquet facilities, and restaurants (including the famed Kon-Tiki Ports, one of the nation's first tiki bars). The top of the structure boasts a large, onion-shaped dome with a small antenna. It was built as a port for dirigibles, which fell out of fashion after the Hindenburg disaster of 1937, but the dome still provides an interesting addition to Michigan Avenue's aerial profile.

The pool has always been the crown jewel of the Medinah facility. Built on the 14th floor and holding 120,000 gallons of water, it was an engineering marvel in its day. The pool is overlooked by two balconies, covered by a huge, intricate ceiling of wooden trestles, and surrounded by a wall of dark blue Spanish Majolica tiles; the quality of its craftsmanship and materials would be difficult to duplicate today. Shortly after it was built, the Medinah pool hosted AAU and other amateur swimming and diving events. Spectators watched from three levels of galleries along the west side of the pool. Many of them came to marvel at Johnny Weissmuller, who trained at the facility, which was then the only 25-yard, indoor pool in the downtown area. Weissmuller, a graduate of Lane Tech High School, won five Olympic Gold medals (and later starred in 12 Tarzan films). During his amateur career, he won 57 events and never lost a race.

The Great Depression gradually ended much of the athletic fanfare of the Medinah Athletic Club. During World War II, the building was used by the USO to entertain troops. Shortly thereafter, it became a hotel. In 1961, a newer wing was added to what was then the Sheridan Hotel. During all these years, the pool was used for hotel guests. In 1981, the Radisson chain purchased the hotel.

Even though time has taken the 1920s splendor from the building, the pool area remained (and remains) magnificent. Another Olympic swimmer, Bill Mulliken, winner of a bronze medal in the 1960 Olympics in Rome, trained there regularly. Former boxing champion Sugar Ray Leonard was spotted jumping rope in the pool's galleries, and singer Donovan Leach, of "Mellow Yellow" and "Sunshine Superman" fame, often sat gazing at its deep blue waters. Mystery writer Sara Paretsky and future Cook County Commissioner Forrest Claypool were also regulars.

The most notable of more recent celebrities may be Tennessee Williams. Like *The Night of the Iguana*'s Reverend T. Lawrence Shannon returning to the Pacific Ocean, Williams regularly sought refuge from a hostile, critical world by coming to the pool. He began visiting Chicago regularly in the late 1970s. The Goodman Theatre's production of his final play, *A House Not Meant to Stand*, brought him to Chicago full time in 1981. That was the same year I graduated from lifeguard school. The lamination was still setting on my Red Cross card when I got a job guarding the pool. Perhaps my second or third day on the job, Tennessee Williams walked in.

Williams wasn't a dashing, fedora-wearing, Pulitzer-Prize-winning-playwright-sunning-with-Truman-Capote-on-the-Mediterranean type anymore. Forty years of heavy drinking and drug use had ravaged his body and his mind. This was reflected in his swimming, as he would regularly disappear under water for long periods at a time. As a teenage lifeguard, I was petrified. What if America's greatest playwright were to drown while I was guarding the pool? After awhile I learned that was just the way he swam, by submerging himself under water while he moved forward with a type of odd dog paddle, coming up for air, and going under again, inching along for what seemed like hours. Other lap swimmers complained to me about him. One advertising copywriter bellowed out, "That crazy old man is ruining my swim. I am working on a Band-Aid slogan and he is stifling my creativity!" Another ad exec with a touch more humility responded, "That crazy old man is Tennessee Williams. I read his plays in high school and college. I think he won a Pulitzer Prize too."

As time wore on, I took the role of one of his many caretakers while he was at the pool. Williams was usually in a walking stupor. He would sit on his glasses, run into doors, and forget to put on his swim trunks and walk into the pool area naked. There were also times when he would become lucid. This seemed to happen on Sunday evenings around supper time. The pool was usually empty, and I would pull up a cabana chair next to him. He would gaze into the blue water and, as if looking into a crystal ball, his memory would return. He always spoke about Broadway in the 1940s, rarely mentioning the Hollywood days of Marlon Brando, Elizabeth Taylor, and Richard Burton. He did speak fondly of Joanne Woodward, saying that she was one of the most brilliant and talented people he had ever seen, and that it was a shame she had given up much of her own acting career in deference to her husband, Paul Newman. He also talked fondly of Chicago, especially the critics: "New York is a mean place. Chicago is much friendlier."

After closing, the pool hosted special parties and events. The most notable of these may have been a Wicca convention, where most of the participants shed their clothing. The next day an angry "warlock," apparently unhappy with his performance the night before, smashed the front window of the pool's entrance with a snake-headed cane and put a hex on the structure.

In 1986, the hotel underwent a five-year renovation process. Now part of the InterContinental chain, the building has been restored to its 1920s magnificence with the addition of all the modern amenities. Aside from a fresh coat of paint and the renovation of the terra cotta Neptune's Fountain that overlooks the east side of the natatorium, little was changed in the pool area itself. A state of the art health club, with the newest in treadmills, saunas, and locker room facilities, has been added. Non-guests can use the pool and health club at yearly rates, or a $15 daily guest fee. The pool and health club is one of the city's great recreational secrets. Many people think that it is private, so it is almost never crowded except during the early morning and just after work. Imagine: $15 buys you not only a tour of one of Chicago's historic architectural gems, but an afternoon of working out, swimming, and sauna bathing in the same deep blue waters and ornate tile surroundings that Johnny Weissmuller, Tennessee Williams, and so many other stars have found refuge from a world that is not always so kind to strangers.

THE INTERCONTINENTAL CHICAGO IS ONE building north of the **Chicago Tribune Tower** (see Oldest Newspaper, p. 18), completed in 1925. Its neo-Gothic grace is visible from a distance, but another distinguishing feature must be seen up close: Embedded in the lower portions of the exterior walls are stones taken from such structures as the Taj Mahal, the Alamo, the Great Wall of China, the Parthenon, the Berlin Wall, and many more (plaques reveal their origins).

 CHIAPPETTI LAMB AND VEAL
3900 S. Emerald Avenue
(1928)

It is just past dawn, and a man in a white lab coat and hard hat is standing in the back of a semi-trailer. Gently waving a small, whip-like stick, he shouts and whistles as the confused lambs exit the trailer and are herded into small wooden pens. As they quietly drink water and munch hay, the lambs do not notice that new townhomes, the Dan Ryan Expressway, and U.S. Cellular Field surround them. Every morning at dawn, semi-trucks deliver more than 1,500 lambs from states like Nebraska, Iowa, and Colorado. Chiappetti Lamb and Veal was once an empire that employed over 40,000 people, processed over nine million animals a year, and covered almost two square miles. Today, Chiappetti Lamb and Veal is the city's oldest, and last, slaughterhouse.

The business began over 75 years ago when Italian immigrant Fiore Chiappetti opened his own butcher shop. While the Chicago's stockyards were known as "hog butcher of the world," and the place where "steak is king," Chiappetti carved out a niche for himself selling lamb to the Jewish, Greek, and Italian immigrants on the near West Side. "We used to have to bid against the big companies like the Armours, Swifts, and Wilsons," says Franco Chiappetti, who represents the fourth generation working for the company. "They used to call people like us alley rats."

That was in the days of Upton Sinclair's *The Jungle*, when the stockyards covered an area bounded by Halsted Street on the east, Ashland Avenue on the west, 39th Street on the north, and 47th Street on south. "When I was a kid this was like a city unto itself, with hundreds of trucks, its own train line, and guys on horseback riding herd throughout the area," Dennis Chiappetti says. "I remember that, and, of course, the smell." Those who were alive then will never forget that smell, which many say drifted all the way to the North Side on hot summer nights. For those who weren't around, imagine opening a pound of bacon that has been sitting in a plastic bag in the hot sun for a week and multiply it by a hundred.

The company expanded to its present location in 1961. In 1971, the Chicago's stockyards closed, as most of the major players moved to smaller towns in Iowa, Nebraska, and spots along the U.S.-Mexico border for more space, cheaper land, and fewer regulations. Chiappetti Lamb and Veal survived. "We had a little niche in the local ethnic market, relationships with stores like Dominick's and kosher butcher shops and local restaurants who had been our customers for years," Chiappetti explains.

The business then weathered the "anti-red meat" trend of the late 1980s by offering ready-to-grill sausages and "case ready" roasts complete with their own thermometers, which appealed to the modern household. But just as in the days of Sandburg, when the stockyards sold "everything but the squeal," lamb by-products are sold for pet food and the hides are removed by hand and sold to tanneries. This efficiency and the new interest in gourmet cooking and foods has allowed Chiappetti Lamb and Veal to make plans for expanding to a new building a few blocks away at 3800 South Morgan Street. There, it will continue to uphold Chicago's "killing floor" tradition.

THE STOCKYARDS MIGHT BE GONE, BUT the "Hog Butcher of the World" tradition still thrives on the wholesale and retail level in the Back of the Yards/south Bridgeport neighborhood. **Allen Brothers** (3737 S. Halsted St., www.allenbrothers.com) has been a Chicago butcher since 1893. What began as a small, storefront shack is now a national and international distributor of some of the finest USDA Prime and gourmet meats available to the general public, mostly through the internet. Their specialties include filet mignon, aged Kobe Wagyu Beef, smoked prime rib, coffee-rubbed smoked beef, and wet- and dry-aged steaks, as well as lamb, duck, and even buffalo meat. **Fontanini Meats** (911 W. 37th Pl., www.fontanini. com) specializes in other types of old-time Chicago signature meats—Italian beef and Italian sausage. They also sell smoked kielbasa, Cajun sausage, breakfast sausages, and fully cooked pot roasts and meatloaf. Like Allen Brothers, Fontanini is more of a wholesale outlet; retail customers can order products through their website.

OLDEST MOVIE THEATER

MUSIC BOX THEATRE
3733 N. Southport Avenue
(1929)

It's no coincidence that as people flocked to the suburbs and bought TV sets in 1950s and 1960s, hundreds of neighborhood theaters throughout Chicago shut down. Some of the large downtown and neighborhood movie palaces like the State and Lake, the United Artists, the Oriental, the Century, the Uptown, and the Granada managed to hold on a bit longer than their smaller counterparts, but are now too the sites of shopping centers, senior homes, or other uses.

The Music Box is one of the few that kept on going, and it is now one of the premier art houses in the country and a distributor of films. Like many theaters, its fortunes were tied to its neighborhood, Lakeview. In the 1970s and early 1980s, the area was gang infested, and like many urban theaters, the Music Box eked through by showing Spanish, Arabic, and other foreign-language films. In 1984, the long-dormant Cubs won a division championship. As Wrigley Field saw the long-empty $1.75 bleacher and $5.00 grandstand seats begin to fill up, gym shoes hanging from telephone wires and gang graffiti began to disappear. Just a year before in 1983, following the lead of the Parkway on North Clark Street, the theater started showing art films from abroad, classic films from the 1940s (such as a double feature of *High Sierra* and *The Maltese Falcon*), and campy musicals that appealed to the young artist, student, and gay populations that were moving into the area. Now, 25 years later, the Music Box is open seven days a week and shows over three hundred films a year.

The Music Box was built in 1929, at the end of the movie palace era, without the grand, terra cotta exterior or the lavish lobbies of some of the downtown and neighborhood film castles. *Theatre Architecture Magazine* wrote that "the theatre represents the smaller, though charming and well equipped, sound picture theatre which is rapidly taking the place of the 'deluxe' palace." The theater was built at a cost of $110,000 and seated eight hundred people. One of its greatest features, which you can still see today, is a deep blue ceiling with scattered twinkling lights for the impression of a moonlit sky. *Tribune* architecture critic Paul Gapp described it as "an eclectic mélange of Italian, Spanish and Pardon-My-Fantasy put together with passion." It has the old Hollywood, Italianate feel of a 1920s set of *Romeo and Juliet*.

According to the Music Box website, the architecture isn't the only thing that has remained from the 1920s. The Music Box is supposedly haunted by a ghost named Whitey. In his life, Whitey managed the theater from 1929 to 1977. He sold tickets, swept the floors, ordered films, hired and fired countless employees, and raised a family two blocks away. He watched as films soared from the bi-planes of *Wings* and *Hell's Angels*, through the turbo-prop planes of Bogart's *Casablanca* and Gables's *Command Decision*, to the "Jets" of both *West Side Story* and John Wayne's *Green*

Berets. Whitey died on Thanksgiving Day 1977, the year that the outer space adventure *Star Wars* transformed the film industry. With all this great film history, it is no wonder that Whitey does not want to leave. Employees and longtime customers say that he can still be seen pacing the aisles or protecting the alley doors so kids can't sneak in.

Today, the Music Box, once "the little theater that could," is not only the oldest, but the largest single movie theater space (not a multiplex) operating full time in the city. Owned by Southport Music Box Corporation, it also distributes foreign and independent films in the theatrical, DVD, and television markets throughout the United States. Surrounded by restaurants, cafés, live theater, bookstores, and nearby Wrigley Field, it has become a highlight in one of the most vibrant areas of the city.

DO THE SUNDAY SHOWINGS OF OLD MUsicals like *Singing in the Rain* and *The Sound of Music* at the Music Box give you the itch for nostalgia? Then a trip to **Yesterday's** (1143 W. Addison St., 773/248-8087) may be just what the doctor ordered. Housed in an old, leaning, yellow sided and tarpaper shack that was built in the 1880s, Yesterday's motto is "Where the past meets the present." Inside you can find everything from old movie stills, hundreds of movie posters, comic books, comic book character posters, dolls, and more. Located just two blocks west of Wrigley Field (see p. 123), it is also the center for Cubs memorabilia, including pennants, hats, photos, posters, framed collections of ticket stubs, and over 3,200 baseball cards. Wait, there's more! Yesterday's is also the place to purchase Elvis stuff, 60s and 70s era board games, lunch boxes, old *TV Guides*, and hundreds of magazines, campaign buttons, election memorabilia and…more. Prices range from a couple of dollars to a few hundred dollars and up. Visit yesterday today.

OLDEST AUTO REPAIR AND BODY SHOP

ERIE-LA SALLE BODY SHOP
146 W. Erie Street
(1934)

It will always be known by its neon sign. With a tail-finned, rounded-hood 1950s sedan bathed in orange, green, and bright red neon lights, you almost expect to see Marilyn Monroe riding in the back seat. For 74 years, cars—Packards, Studebakers, Buicks, Ford Chevys, and Cadillacs—have rolled underneath this sign to be repaired.

These repairs have been overseen by the Gottfred family, owners of the Erie-La Salle Body Shop for three generations. According to the Body Shop's website, this run makes it "the longest continuously owned repair shop of its kind in the state of Illinois." When the family first started, dents were repaired with mallets, and painting was done simply, often by hand. World War II brought in new technologies such as high-pressure paint sprayers and fast-drying lacquers and enamels. The introduction of plastics and fiberglass brought even more improvements to the industry. Acrylic resin-based materials such as *bondo* allowed small dents to be filled with the pliable, clay-like substance, eliminating the need to replace entire sections of a vehicle (though this was only possible after the application of several coats and hours of fine sanding). In the last ten years, however, the cost of labor has made this type of repair cost prohibitive. Now, computer-based applications such as A.D.P. estimating software, photo imaging, and digital imaging are being applied to the trade. As for the neon sign, that hasn't changed. Let us hope it keeps lighting up La Salle Street for generations to come.

WANT TO BUY SOMEBODY SOME FLOWERS to cheer them up while their car gets fixed or your car gets fixed? **LaSalle Flower Shop** (731 N. La Salle St., 312/787-3680), basically across the street from the body shop, has been selling flowers at this location since 1935. Walk inside and you'll see the glass cases and molded ceiling of Old Chicago. It also has a very cool neon sign featuring a red rose on a green background, slightly tilted ever since a nearby lamppost was hit by a car, sending it crashing into the sign. Some may tell you that this was the flower shop where Irish gangster and Al Capone's nemesis Dion O' Banion was shot, but that occurred at Schofield's Flower Shop, which was two blocks east, closer to the Holy Name Cathedral, and is long gone.

OLDEST HOT DOG STAND

JIM'S ORIGINAL MAXWELL STREET
1250 S. Union Avenue
(1939)

Much has been written about the Chicago style hot dog. A Vienna sausage inundated with an avalanche of mustard, onions, relish, tomato, pickles, cucumbers, and sport peppers, is as much a part of Chicago as Lake Michigan. The lore surrounding Chicago's open air Maxwell Street Market rivals that of our hot dog, so it is only fitting that the story of Jim's Original Maxwell Street combines the two.

Jim's Original Maxwell Street now stands at 1250 South Union Avenue, only a block from its original location. It was moved there after a period of controversy and urban renewal that led to the destruction of the entire Maxwell Street neighborhood in favor of new housing and shopping developments. Sure, Jim's still sells bone-in, pork chop sandwiches, Polish sausages smothered with grilled onions, and the famous Chicago red hots. But somehow they just don't taste the same. To really understand what it was like to eat a Jim's Original, you have to know the history of Maxwell Street itself.

Named for Dr. Phillip Maxwell, Maxwell Street originated in 1847 as a wooden plank road that ran from the South Branch of the Chicago River to Blue Island. From its origins until the early part of the twenty-first century, Maxwell Street was a popular destination for new immigrants. Chuck Cowdery, past president of the Maxwell Street Coalition, compared it to Ellis Island, but took it a step further. "Ellis Island was a processing center while Maxwell Street was a neighborhood where new arrivals not only came, but found work, housing, clothing, food, family, and friends old and new."

The first arrivals to the neighborhood were Irish. Germans, Greeks, Bohemians, and Italians settled the area well into the twentieth century. But it was the Jews from Eastern Europe who brought their two-thousand-year-old tradition of trade to the area. Like the markets they established in Prague, Moscow, and Warsaw, the Jews made the Maxwell Street Market come alive. The wide streets were filled with pushcarts, makeshift wooden stands, and later buildings with stores. Whether you wanted fruit, meat, books, tools, clothes, shoes, furniture, bikes, auto parts, or even cars, you could buy it on Maxwell Street. But unlike today's Wal-Marts, the prices were not listed on bar codes. It was a place of barter, where everything was negotiable. If a possible buyer walked away from a vendor because he did not have the cash to pay the asking price, the seller, noticing a roll from the U.S. Postal Service likely replied, "Don't worry if you don't have enough money. I take stamps." It was into this atmosphere that Jimmy Stefanovic arrived in 1939.

A native of Macedonia, Jimmy Stefanic fled Russia amid the violence and terror of the 1919 Russian Revolution. "We want to travel to the Rumanian border to get to Yugoslavia," Stefanovic says. "But it takes us one hundred days to walk 25 kilometers. Why? Fighting, fighting. War, fighting. Oh guns. Night and day guns."

Stefanovic, who may have sold more hot dogs than anyone outside of Nathan's on Coney Island, credits a dog for saving his life. "My uncle had a big dog named Doruff, he was trained good," Stefanovic says in the book, *Maxwell Street: Survival in a Bazaar*, written by Ira Berkow. "My father take Doruff, put message around his neck and with some gold pieces, and tell him, go to friends in Rumanian town across the river to get bread. Before you know it, he comes back with basket of bread around his neck. We do this 25 times. Doruff save our life…. One night, Doruff comes back, he has blood all over. They shot the dog. He return to us and then lay down. Everybody was cry."

Stefanovic ended up settling in Chicago. At first he sold taffy apples. His aunt owned a hot dog stand at Halsted and Maxwell, making Jim's Original Maxwell Street even older than the 1939 date by some accounts. As his aunt was getting up in years, Jimmy bought it from her for $280. He worked 12 hours a day to build up the stand, but Stefanovic also benefited from the era. By 1939, the Depression was coming to a close. World War II, with its shortages of supplies and rationing of staples, brought new importance to Maxwell Street's underground economy. Then World War II ended, and the economy of the entire nation soared.

African-Americans helped to revitalize Maxwell Street after the war. Although they had been relocating to Chicago since the 1920s, the post-war migration from the South to Chicago became the largest influx ever. Many of the newcomers from Mississippi, Tennessee, and Alabama settled in the Maxwell Street area. One of these settlers was McKinley Morganfield, better known as Muddy Waters. Another was harmonica king Little Walter. The two met one afternoon when Waters, who often performed on Maxwell Street, was "walking through Jewtown [slang for Maxwell Street] when I heard this crazy harmonica. I just had to stop and listen."

Maxwell Street became a blues mecca during the 1950s, 60s, and into the 1970s. Some of area's better known performers included Waters and Little Walter, as well as Buddy Guy, J.B. Hutto, and Hound Dog Taylor. As time wore on major performers became too established to play for tips, but local characters like Maxwell Street Jimmy Davis and the Black Lone Ranger kept the street's blues tradition alive.

Jimmy Stefanovic rode this wave of prosperity through the 1950s, '60s, and '70s. One Labor Day weekend Jim's Original Maxwell Street sold roughly twenty thousand red hots and Polish sausages. Jim's became famous worldwide! People came from all over the world to sample a Chicago hot dog or a Maxwell Street Polish, as they do for our pizza.

In 1967, the University of Illinois at Chicago expanded its campus south of Roosevelt Road. Subsidized housing also cut off Maxwell's western end at Morgan Street. This was a harbinger of things to come. The 1970s and early 1980s saw some deterioration in the Maxwell Street Market. However, the market was still successful. New items like CDs and pornographic videos replaced some of the old staples. As a place where newcomers without much money could establish a small business, Maxwell Street still attracted immigrants. During the mid-1990s, the entire market was moved west towards the train tracks, and was only opened during regulated hours on weekends. The Maxwell Street neighborhood, with its many historic buildings, was slated for demolition.

Groups like the Maxwell Street Coalition battled Mayor Daley to keep the area open. They were joined by the Landmarks Preservation Council, and artists and blues musicians throughout the city, including Bo Diddley, who held a fundraiser to save the area. Maxwell Street historians lovingly point to the phrase, "the place where the only color that mattered was green," as an example of the racial harmony that dominated the area. Ironically, this very phrase had another meaning, as the area was demolished in favor of high-end condominiums, UIC student highrises, strip malls, and a parking garage.

One of the few remnants of the original area is Jim's Original Maxwell Street. It was kept open through a series of protests. Bruce King, president of the Culinary Historians of Chicago, wrote: "I am strongly in support of the efforts to preserve one of Chicago's important cultural landmarks, Jim's hot dog stand at the corner of Maxwell and Halsted Streets. As an historian of food and food ways with a special interest in both food and ethnicity, I can attest to the significance of the Maxwell Street area and Jim's place in it. In delivering papers and speeches on these subjects across the country, Jim's is always at the center of these discussions. The talks and pictures unfailingly stir great interest in both the academic and cultural audiences.... Vienna Beef's Maxwell Street posters can be seen wherever the product is sold across the United States and in Europe. These 'lowly' sausages mean 'Chicago' to many outside the city. They are important parts of the city's culture and history...and that means Jim's, a stand that has existed since the 1920s."

Jim's was moved a block east to 1220 South Union Avenue. Many thought it would end there. To make matters worse, another hot dog stand, Maxwell Street Express, was moved right next door. It was hoped that the move and the competition would open even more land for developers, but Jim's has survived. After all, you are not a true Chicagoan until you have had a Chicago hot dog, a Polish with onions, or a pork chop sand-wich from Jim's—preferably for breakfast.

☞ ONCE IN THE HEART OF THE MAXWELL Street district, the area around Jimmy's still features a few holdovers from the old days. If you need socks, you can always find, **"the sock man,"** offering giant bags of socks for $6–$7, depending on your bargaining skills. The demolition of the old Maxwell has led to the erection of "University Village," a suburbanesque community filled with bars, restaurants, and a **Barbara's Bookstore** (1218 S. Halsted St., 312/413-2665).

OLDEST DINER

WHITE PALACE GRILL
1159 S. Canal Street
(1939)

t is midnight at the White Palace Grill, and the restaurant is filled with security guards, truck drivers, Metra employees, and couples, all huddled over cups of warm coffee. A menu card advertises over one hundred items, including grilled Grecian tilapia and shrimp salads. Most of the regulars are content to chow down on fried eggs, hash browns, and chicken fried steak while sipping coffee and bobbing their heads to tunes like Jr. Walker and the All Stars' "Shotgun."

In recent years, townhouse developments and mega-franchises like Home Depot, Staples, and Bed, Bath, and Beyond have changed the face of this South Maxwell Street area. Luckily, Chernin's Shoes, Manny's Deli, the White Palace Grill, and other businesses maintain the area's melting pot tradition.

The Bookman family opened the White Palace Grill in 1939. The restaurant is not officially a diner. Diners are named after dining cars that were abandoned by the railroads during the 1920s and turned into restaurants after the Depression; the White Palace is a solid brick building. With the glowing, white sign, the nearby train tracks, truck depots, and the Chicago skyline looming behind it, the White Palace Grill sits atop the Chicago heap. May the hot coffee, patty melts, and apple pie never the leave its white Formica counter, except in the belly of a satisfied customer.

☞ THE WHITE PALACE GRILL IS PERFECTLY situated for a Sunday morning visit to the **"new" Maxwell Street market** (Roosevelt Rd. & Canal St.). The glory days of bluesmen like Muddy Waters playing at the original Maxwell Street three blocks south are long gone, but Sunday morning shoppers can still find everything from tools to TVs, tires, CDs, shoes, electronics, and now computer parts and software in this newer, somewhat cleaner version of the market. There are also produce and spice stands, and several sit-down Mexican food booths (perfect at 7 AM!). The market is in session every Sunday morning and it opens early, before dawn, and the action usually winds down around noon—rain, shine, snow, or sleet. There is no better way to start off a trip to Maxwell than a giant, pre-dawn breakfast of eggs, sausages, potatoes, and coffee (for about seven bucks) at the White Palace.

PIZZERIA UNO
29 E. Ohio Street
(1943)

As much as sailboats along the lakefront or the Magnificent Mile have come to symbolize the Windy City, so too has the image of a steel spatula under a slice of deep-dish pizza, melted cheese stretching as it's served. Chicago may be "the second city" but it is the first city of pizza.

We owe our thanks for the innovation of deep-dish pizza to Pizzeria Uno, the city's oldest pizza parlor. Pizzeria Uno at 29 East Ohio Street is a Chicago legend. It started as a novel idea in the cavernous basement of a downtown mansion, and is now a corporation with over 200 franchises in 30 states, Puerto Rico, South Korea, and the United Arab Emirates.

Texas native Ike Sewell opened the first restaurant on the corner of Ohio and Wabash in 1943. Unos.com states that "Americans ate pizza primarily as a snack. But Ike figured that if you combined some of the ingredients with impressive quantities of the finest meats, fresh chesses, ripe vegetables, and flavorful spices, pizza would become a meal. This was the start of deep dish pizza." Others dispute this story of America's first deep dish pizza recipe. The website fails to mention that Sewell was the bar manager at Riccardo's, the former River North hangout for writers, reporters, and artists. Older versions of the Uno's story state that Sewell and Ric Riccardo were partners when they opened Pizzeria Uno. But the greatest discrepancy involves Rudy Malnati. A 1956 *Chicago Daily News* article credits Malnati, who was Uno's head cook, with inventing the first deep-dish pizza recipe. In today's world of the internet, the Food Channel, and the billion-dollar cookbook industry, it quite possible that somebody who is not of an ethnic heritage can become a chef of its cuisine—just look at Rick Bayless. However, in 1943, pizza—and for that matter spaghetti, tomato sauce, Italian sausage, or mozzarella cheese—was almost completely unheard of in the United States. Outside of a few urban Italian neighborhoods, you couldn't even buy the ingredients. So it makes more sense that somebody of Italian heritage would have had to play some part in the invention of deep-dish pizza. Today, Rudy's son Lou runs the deep-dish pizza chain Lou Malnati's. Like Pizzeria Uno, it is franchised throughout the country. Lou Malnati's pizza tastes remarkably similar to Pizzeria Uno's.

The story of who brought the first pizza to the United States is also disputed. Pizza existed in some form even before Christ, as Virgil's Aeneid mentions flat cakes of bread covered with cheese. In 1522, tomatoes were brought to Italy from Peru, and when the natives of the Naples region added them to bread, cheese, and olive oil, the first true pizzas were born. Chicago's

Taylor Street area has long been a destination for Neapolitan immigrants. Old-timers from the area claim that their grandparents told stories of men pushing homemade carts by Taylor and Racine as early as the 1890s. Fashioned from copper washtubs, the carts had small bits of charcoal underneath. This kept the two-cent pies made of cheese, tomato, and olive oil hot. Others dispute the claim that anyone sold pizza in Chicago then. The nation's first and oldest documented pizza parlor is Gennaro Lombardi's on New York's Spring Street, which opened its doors in 1905. Others from the large Italian community in New Haven, Connecticut, also claim some credit for the invention of the famous pie.

Another local pizza first is the invention of frozen pizza. The Home Run Inn was originally a bar at the intersection 31st and Kildare in Chicago. Nick Perrino, the son of the first owners and a veteran of World War II, decided to serve a thin crust pie to hungry bar customers in 1947. The idea was so popular that the family could no longer keep up with orders. In order to facilitate faster production, the pizzas were first refrigerated and then frozen ahead of time. One day somebody took one of the pizzas home, threw it in the oven, and the rest, as they say, is history.

One thing that's for certain is that whenever Chicago and food are mentioned  in the same sentence, deep-dish pizza is part of the conversation, and we can all thank Pizzeria Uno for that.

TREE STUDIOS (601–623 N. STATE ST.; 4–10 E. Ohio St.; 3–7 E. Ontario St.) was designed as a bohemian haven. Complete with a courtyard for sketching and large windows facing east to absorb the best light, many of the apartments were designed specifically for visual artists. Begun in 1894 (two annexes were added in 1912 and 1913) by philanthropists Judge Lambert Tree and his wife Anne, the owners provided stipends for artists provided that they created work. And it paid off. Just a few of the famous artists who have created and lived at Tree Studios include painter Ruth Van Sickle Ford, sculptor John Storrs, and actors Peter Falk and Burgess Meredith. The complex was listed on the National Register of Historic Places on December 16, 1974, and the State Street building was listed as a Chicago landmark on February 26, 1997. The buildings have since been restored and modernized by a major developer. Unfortunately, they're now occupied by businesses and offices.

OLDEST SOUL FOOD RESTAURANT

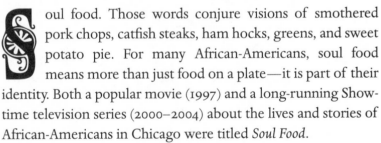

ARMY AND LOU'S
422 E. 75th Street
(1945)

oul food. Those words conjure visions of smothered pork chops, catfish steaks, ham hocks, greens, and sweet potato pie. For many African-Americans, soul food means more than just food on a plate—it is part of their identity. Both a popular movie (1997) and a long-running Showtime television series (2000–2004) about the lives and stories of African-Americans in Chicago were titled *Soul Food*.

Even though Chicago has seen some famous soul food restaurants like Catfish Digby's and the Soul Queen, the oldest and most celebrated soul food restaurant in the city is Army and Lou's. Established in 1945 by William Armstrong (Army) and his wife Luvilla (Lou), Army and Lou's is the second oldest African-American-owned business in the Midwest. Just as the term "soul food" suggests, more than food is served there; for over half a century, Army and Lou's has been a center for the South Side African-American community. In the area of politics, Mayor Harold Washington used the restaurant as his home base during the divisive days of "Council Wars" in the 1980s. Black entertainers and artists, from jazz musicians to blues, soul, and hip-hop stars, have also used the restaurant's food to energize their acts. "Entertainers like Cab Calloway and later Sammy Davis Jr. used to come to the restaurant all the time," Delores Reynolds, the restaurant's current owner, says. "That was during the restaurant's early days, when Mr. and Mrs. Armstrong owned the restaurant."

Arriving in Chicago before World War II, Mr. and Mrs. Armstrong and many of restaurant's first customers were among the African-Americans who came to Chicago as part of the Great Migration. *The Encyclopedia of Chicago* states that in 1910, Chicago had roughly 44,000 African-Americans. This increased to 492,000 by 1950 and 813,000 by 1960 as African-Americans left their homes in Mississippi, Alabama, Georgia, Louisiana, and other states to come to Chicago. Besides a willingness to work and start a new life, these migrants brought with them their own culture. Jazz, mainly in the form of Louis Armstrong and Jelly Roll Morton, arrived in Chicago via New Orleans in the early 1920s. Most of Chicago's early jazz scene was centered in the historic Bronzeville area, as artists like Louis Armstrong, Fletcher Henderson, Count Basie, and Earl Hines played at the Sunset Café, at 315 West 35th Street, or at rooms like the Chez Paree or the Parkway Ballroom on 47th Street. Author Richard Wright and poet Gwendolyn Brooks lived in Bronzeville as well.

This blend of music, literature, and culture prompted William Armstrong to open a restaurant in 1945. "The restaurant was originally located at 39th and Indiana, in the heart of the Bronzeville area," Reynolds says. "William worked as a writer for the *Chicago Defender* [see Oldest Black Newspaper, p. 98], which at the time was located on 39th Street. But he also had a passion for cooking, so when the restaurant opened it was not only a place to meet, but a place for artists and community leaders to gather and percolate their ideas."

Mr. and Mrs. Armstrong ran the restaurant until 1961, when it was taken over by another couple, Mary and Charles Cole. Unfortunately, urban renewal and economic struggles left much of the historic Bronzeville neighborhood in decay, so the Coles moved Army and Lou's to its current located at 422 East 75th Street. "The Chatham neighborhood was, and has always been, a very stable area," Reynolds says. "The Coles ran the restaurant until 1990. It was during this time that the restaurant continued to be a political center for the community. Mayor Harold Washington, Sixth Ward Alderman Eugene Sawyer [who succeeded Washington as mayor], Jesse Jackson, and many others regularly met here to plot strategy during the 'Council Wars.' Jesse Jackson and Jesse Jackson Jr. are still regular customers."

Another couple bought the restaurant after the Coles retired, but they did not meet with the same success. "They took it over for two years but the restaurant fell into disrepair," Reynolds says. "The South Shore Bank owned it, and I agreed to reopen it in 1992. I approached Mary and Charles Cole, who came back as consultants, and together we were able to restore the restaurant to its former state."

Without missing a beat, the politicians, entertainers, artists, and neighbors once again flocked to Army and Lou's. "The mayor has been here many times, and Governor Blagojevich, former Governor Edgar, Aurelia Pucinski, and other politicians have come around, especially around election time," Reynolds says. Following on the heels of Sammy Davis Jr. and Cab Calloway, a new generation or two of entertainers have also returned to Army and Lou's. "There was a time when Eddie Murphy came in here, and he liked the gumbo so much he had us regularly ship it to him in California," Reynolds says. "Not too long ago, Alicia Keys came in—you should have seen the crowd she drew. The hip hop artist Common also eats here."

In the Armstrongs' tradition, the restaurant has maintained its link to local black culture, promoting neighborhood artists and musicians. "We have artwork on the walls that people can view, as well as buy, from a local gallery in the neighborhood," Reynolds says. "We also feature local jazz artists, just two or three pieces, every Friday night."

It is not the jazz or the artwork that really brings the famous politicians, artists, and regular neighborhood people back to Army and Lou's. Instead, it is 60 years of home-cooked Southern-bred gumbo, mac 'n' cheese, sea perch, catfish nuggets, short ribs, mixed greens, baby back ribs, chitterlings, sweet potato pie, and freshly baked peach and apple cobbler that keeps the doors swinging and the oven singing at 422 East 75th Street.

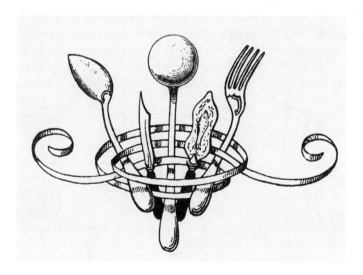

AFTER SATISFYING A SOUL FOOD FIX AT Army and Lou's, you can enjoy a piece of Chicago entertainment history and African-American culture a few blocks east. The **New Regal Theater** (1641 E. 79ᵗʰ St., 312/902-1500) is a landmark in the East Chatham/Avalon Park neighborhood. Legend has it that the architect, John Eberson, got his inspiration for the building from a Persian incense burner. Resembling a Middle Eastern mosque, with onion-shaped domes, spiraling turrets, and perhaps the most elaborate exterior Spanish tilework in the city, the theater was built as the Avalon Theater in 1927. A 2,400-seat structure that rivaled North Side theaters like the Uptown and Granada, it was part of the Warner Brothers circuit in the 1930s and 40s. After bringing all of the major movies and stage shows to the South Side for almost 50 years, the building became the Miracle Temple Church. In 1987, after the original Regal Theater was torn down, the New Regal Theater became a source of pride for the local community. It went through another round of closing and renovation, but re-opened in October of 2007. Since then, first rate soul and R&B acts like Smokey Robinson and The Temptations, as well as community theater and musical productions have all graced the stage at the New Regal.

OLDEST TAMALE SHOP

 LA GUADALUPANA
1365 W. 37th Street
(1945)

Taquerias, carnicerias, and other Mexican American businesses have become as much a part of Chicago's neighborhoods as the corner store and hot dog stand. In 1945, however, the city's ethnic landscape was dominated by Italians, Irish, Germans, Lithuanians, Greeks, and other Europeans. So when Pedro and Lucy Castro began selling tamales and other Mexican food items in 1945, they were ethnic pioneers.

"My grandparents came to Chicago in the early 1940s from Guanajuato, Mexico," Alex Castro, who represents the third generation working at the plant, says. "He started working at La Victoria Bakery on West 46th Place, making tortillas, tamales, and bread. He then opened his own business, La Guadalupana, on Roosevelt Road, where he continued to make baked goods, but began more and more to specialize in masa and tamales."

Although there had been a small Mexican American community centering around Our Lady of Guadalupe Church on the city's Southeast Side, the city's Little Village and Pilsen neighborhoods were still mostly inhabited by Czechoslovakians, Scandinavians, and other European groups. So when the Castros moved La Guadalupana into the area in the early 1960s, they were setting the stage for a Mexican immigrant community that, according the 2000 census, ranks only behind Los Angeles in population size.

"They were one of the first Mexican-American families to settle in Little Village," Castro says. "They took over a building that a Scandinavian family had formerly owned, turning what had been a furniture store into a grocery store."

For the next 40 years Pedro, his wife Lucy, and later their son Rogelio, developed the store from what was truly a mom-and-pop business into what is now a small manufacturing plant that distributes tamales throughout Chicagoland. La Guadalupana makes tamales with pork, chicken, beef, spicy chicken and pork, pepper and cheese, and even with strawberry, pineapple, or coconut fillings. As part of the fastest growing and soon to be largest minority community in the city, La Guadalupana also represents the oldest Mexican-American business in Chicago.

👉 LA GUADALUPANA IS NEAR THE PILSEN neighborhood, which along with Little Village ("La Villita"), is filled with Mexican restaurants, bakeries, and bars. Originally settled by Czechs (hence the name), Pilsen is bounded roughly by Halsted Street (east), Ashland Avenue (west), 18th Street (north), and 22nd Street (south). Some of the many notable eateries are **Nuevo Leon** (1515 W. 18th St.) and the **Birrieria Reyes de Ocatlan** (1322 W. 18th St.). Nuevo Leon is an inexpensive, all-purpose authentic Mexican restaurant with excellent moles. The Birrieria exclusively serves *birria*, goatmeat slowly stewed in clay pots. Topped with onions and cilantro, and simmering in its own juices, it is a delicacy that everybody should try at least once. For a final dose of Mexican culture, art, film, and literature, the **National Museum of Mexican Art** (1852 W. 19th St., 312/738-1503) is the largest Latino museum in the country. The Annual Day of the Dead Exhibit and activities, which run from late September through early November, should not be missed.

OLDEST DRIVE-IN RESTAURANT

SUPERDAWG
6363 N. Milwaukee Avenue
(1948)

ust as the John Hancock Center and the Sears Tower represent the Loop, two giant plastic hot dogs, Maurie and Flaurie, represent the city's Northwest Side.

Bathed in the light from the neon signs below, Maurie and Flaurie are the beacons of Superdawg. As Chicago's oldest and only drive-in restaurant, it is the last link to the era of Bill Haley, Elvis, *American Graffiti*, The Beach Boys, and *Grease* (which was based on events at Taft High School, located only a few blocks away). With drive-in bays, carhops, window trays, and the famous lighted menu and speaker board, Superdawg is indeed the real thing. Although they are vanishing at an alarming rate, some true drive-ins still exist around the country. Superdawg is Zagat rated, has been featured on *Nightline*, *The To-*

day Show, Emeril Live, and PBS's *Hot Dog Program,* and written about in *The New York Times* and the book *1,000 Places to See in the USA and Canada Before You Die.*

It all began with its owners, Maurie and Florence (Flaurie) Berman in 1948. "The original purpose of the business was to get my wife and I through school," Maurie Berman says. "I was a former World War II GI studying to be an accountant and my wife was teaching in the Chicago Public Schools. A lot of vets were operating hot dog carts during the summer to make extra money, so that seemed like a good way to go."

Luckily for Chicagoans, the Bermans, who have now been married for over 60 years, were not content with an ordinary hot dog cart. The concept started with a name: instead of a name like "Maurie's Red Hots" or "Flaurie's Place," the Bermans gave their business the grand moniker of Superdawg. "That was the time when Superman had just become popular, so we came up with the name Superdawg," Berman says. "At first I was fearful that I might be infringing on the copyright, so I wrote to the King Syndicate, which owned Superman at the time, but they didn't respond, so I went ahead with it."

Next, came the building's unique design. Like many drive-ins that were popping up in the west, the Bermans wanted something that would capture the attention of people driving up Milwaukee Avenue. "My original concept was to have the entire restaurant cast in the shape of a hot dog and bun," Berman says. "But the contractors told me that it would cost too much."

Instead, they settled on a more conventional drive-in arrangement, with an added touch. Maurie the giant wiener is clad in a Tarzan-style tunic, flexing his muscles to impress his mate. In true 1950s fashion, the female Flaurie is wide-eyed and amazed, fawning over Maurie. The two of them are perched atop the roof of Superdawg, their eyes blinking like the stoplights along Devon Avenue. "Originally Maurie and Flaurie were made out of papier-mâché, but that only lasted two years," Berman says. "Then we made new ones out of Silastic brand plastic strips, but like the paper, it did not do well in Chicago's harsh weather. The third version, made of hard plastic fared a little better, but the fiberglass seems to have worked the best."

The ear-catching name and eye-catching statues may have helped attract initial customers, but Superdawg has lasted for so long because of the food. There are hundreds of hot dog places in Chicago, and a lot of them serve good red hots. Few can match the Superdawg. The combination of the high quality sausage, the poppy seed bun, the hard dill pickle, the special green relish, and sport peppers results in better taste than your average dog.

"During the 1950s, '60s, and '70s we would travel around the country, driving hundreds of miles out of our way to visit certain places and to see what they were doing with their hot dogs," Berman says. "But we honestly couldn't find anything that inclined us to change."

The french fries are crinkle-cut and then nestled in a colorful, Superdawg character box that people save for home decorations. You can count on prefectly grilled onions on the Superburgers and fries cooked to a crisp finish. Time after time, year after year, you never get soggy fries, hard onions, a chewy red hot, or a Whoopercheesie that is not melted—that's what I call quality control.

Completely remodeled in 2003, today's Superdawg is adorned in flashy neon S's, purple and white triangles, the classic Maurie and Flaurie wiener statues, and a glowing neon crown. Pull into a bay on a warm spring, summer, or fall night, and dine under the neon light and the moonlight with a Superdawg and fries on a tray attached to your car window. When you are done eating, flick the switch and a server will come to your window. It is something residents of Norwood Park, Jefferson Park, and

Edgebrook have done for 60 years, and every Chicagoan should experience at least once.

☞ SUPERDAWG HAS LONG BEEN THE PRIDE and joy of the city's Norwood Park neighborhood. An outpost on the far Northwest Side of the city, there are few notable "oldests" or commercial attractions nearby. Yet the drive-in is literally across the street from the beginning of the North Branch Bike Trail. Starting at Devon and Milwaukee avenues, the trail runs about 20 miles all the way to the **Chicago Botanic Garden** (www.chicagobotanic.org, 847/835-5440) in Glencoe. Most of the trail is tree-lined, and most of it parallels the North Branch of the Chicago River. Along the way you will probably see deer so tame they are seldom startled by unobtrusive bikers, as well as Great Blue herons and other wildlife. And, a Superdawg and fries are the perfect way to reward yourself after 40 miles of biking.

JAZZ RECORD MART
27 E. Illinois Street
(1959)

ost stores simply sell merchandise. But like San Francisco's City Lights Bookstore, Chicago's Jazz Record Mart goes beyond being a retail establishment—it is a cultural institution. Together with Delmark Records, Jazz Record Mart has influenced the national and international sound of jazz and blues. Formerly located in the basement of the Jazz Record Mart, Delmark has released over three hundred jazz and blues records, including the groundbreaking jazz work of the Association for the Advancement of Creative Musicians (AACM), Junior Wells's *Hoodoo Man Blues*, and, most recently, the first album by Reginald R. Robinson, a ragtime piano player who recently won a MacArthur Genius Grant. Jazz Record Mart sells these great records and much more. The store is practically a museum and collectors travel from all over the world to get rare and out of print recordings that aren't available elsewhere.

The owner of Jazz Record Mart tells the story of its creation: "When I moved here in 1958, I began selling records out of what was a commercial apartment. Then in 1959, the owner of what was then called Seymour's Record Mart at 439 South Wabash was getting on in years and decided to sell it. John Steiner was going to sell me Belmont Records, a 1920s jazz and blues label. He loaned me the money to buy Seymour's, which was then in the Auditorium Building for $1,500. It was a shell of a store, but from that time on I stopped missing meals, at least regularly. Because of my desire to record the old music, the owner thought I would be the right person to have it. He said he would make it feasible. He knew I didn't have a lot of capital and he'd help out. I had that letter on the wall, just a one-paragraph letter. It ended: 'Get going young fellow.' That was my motto."

Since 1959, the store has moved from the intersection of Wabash and Chicago to 7 West Grand Avenue, 11 West Grand Avenue, 444 North Wabash Avenue, and its current location around the corner at 27 East Illinois Street. Even though the outside may have changed, the inside has remained a time machine. Unlike other music stores, the JRM looks like a collector's basement full of old posters, banners, and signs made with magic markers. It is the urban equivalent of an old general store where virtually every inch from floor to ceiling is filled with anything you could ever want. Dozens of dusty white bins are filled with CDs featuring early jazz giants Louis Armstrong and King Oliver, the bebop of Charlie Parker, the blues of Muddy Waters, Sleepy John Estes, and Magic Sam, and over ten thousand others. The store also offers recent releases and imported collector CDs. It has sections devoted to vinyl records and 78s. JRM sells jazz and blues books, documentary and concert DVDs, videos, cassettes, posters, postcards, sweatshirts, and t-shirts.

Browsing through these bins is a mini–history course. The yellowing cover portraits transform from the black and white photos and ink drawings of the 1930s and 40s to the Technicolor-style covers of the 1950s to the bold AACM-era cover art of the 1960s and 70s. The music inside changes just as much as the cover art—from Benny Goodman in the 1930s to Stan Getz and Dizzy Gillespie in the 1950s to Miles Davis in the 1960s.

Many famous figures in the jazz and blues world have made the Jazz Record Mart their day job. Among the most notable are Joe Segal, who worked at Seymour's before opening his legendary club, Jazz Showcase; guitarist Mike Bloomfield; harmonica ace Charlie Musselwhite; Jim O'Neil, who went on to become founder of *Living Blues* magazine; and Bruce Iglauer, the founder and president of Alligator Records.

"The Jazz Record Mart was like a bridge between the blues world on the South and West Sides and the growing world of white international blues fans who hung out at the Jazz Record Mart, who came here to find out about gigs, musicians," says Iglauer. "There were little signs, pieces of paper taped to the walls about various gigs at ghetto taverns. It was an incredible flow of musicians through there because it was one of the few ways that they could get a break. There weren't a lot of companies recording Chicago blues at that time, so musicians came to hang out at the Jazz Record Mart in hopes of attracting attention." The combination of Koester's knowledge, Delmark's recordings, and the Jazz Record Mart's position as gathering spot and clubhouse for artists and fans made the JRM the perfect distribution point. "Jazz goes through changes, but the new style doesn't replace the old style, except chronologically," Koester says in the documentary film, *A Tribute to Delmark*. "In 1965 I knew that I was not going to find another Louis Armstrong, and Charlie Parker was still the most important artist, but he had been dead for ten years. I was aware that there were changes in jazz, but the test was what did these new guys think of the artists who had come before them? They all knew about and admired, even idolized, the work of people like Louis Armstrong, so I knew that they were probably right on."

Delmark went on to record the jazz of artists Roscoe Mitchell, Malachi Favors, Lester Bowie, Anthony Braxton, and others who would eventually begin the avant-garde jazz movement of the 1960s, which changed the face of jazz worldwide. "It's kind of funny," Koester says. "It is over 40 years later and they are still calling it the avant-garde, or new music, so I guess I must have done something."

Koester also recorded hundreds of blues and folk blues albums. The most notable of these is Junior Wells's *Hoodoo Man Blues*. A stellar seller to this day, it followed the path of rock and rollers as not a collection of singles but rather as a long-playing work with a cohesive theme and style. "Up until that time, bluesmen would record singles of two and half or so minutes, which would then be put out a longer format as basically a collection of songs," Koester says. "With *Hoodoo Man* there were no time restrictions on any of the songs, so in that way it was the first time a blues artist had put out what we now call an album."

Most of these records were pressed, stored, and archived in the basement of the Jazz Record Mart. During the 1970s, Delmark expanded to a new building on North Lincoln Avenue, and Koester began to spend less time working and managing at the Mart. That was a mistake, he says. "I hired the wrong guy to manage my store," Koester says. "He had his own agenda. He was planning on opening a store, and he was turning my employees and my customers and some of my suppliers against me. He was deliberately over-ordering. Little things like that. He came close to putting me out of business."

Koester hung on. His store stays alive while most CD stores are dying like mosquitoes trapped in a sudden frost. Part of this success is due to a loyal clientele. Unlike ordering things on the internet, going to the Jazz Record Mart is an excursion. At JRM, you can read about a new artist, start up a conversation with a fan, or run into a celebrity like John Cusack, who regularly shops at the JRM. You can wander through and see, feel, touch, and even smell the history of jazz and blues.

"Most record stores think only about moving product, and they hire marketing people and do computer inventory so that they can constantly change their displays and jerk something off the shelf as soon as it proves to not be cost-effective," Koester says. "I run the Jazz Record Mart with my heart, and see it as a place where the music is not only sold, but preserved so it can be available to future generations."

UNLIKE NEW ORLEANS, CHICAGO DOES not have a "jazz district"; clubs are scattered throughout the city. A couple Chicago favorites, luckily, are a short walk from the Jazz Record Mart. **Andy's** (11 E. Hubbard St., 312/642-6805), which has live jazz seven nights a week, is about three blocks southeast. The entertainment there might be anything from Dixieland, piano trios, and hard bop to jam sessions and out-of-town guests. For blues fans, **Blue Chicago** (536 N. Clark St., 312/661-0100) is a couple blocks west of the Jazz Record Mart. Experience the music live, then take it home on CD or vinyl from the JRM.

III. The Suburbs and Exurbs

OLDEST BAR

 GLENVIEW HOUSE
1843 Glenview Road
Glenview (1878)

America was settled largely by Puritans, whose beliefs in temperance still influence much of the politics of the nation's heartland today. So when German and Irish immigrants began arriving in the United States in the 1840s and 1850s, clashes in culture abounded. A large number of the disputes, such as Chicago's lager beer riots, involved drinking and saloons. For many northern European immigrants, the town's social, political, and cultural life revolved around the saloon. This was definitely the role of the Glenview House. Opened in 1878, it began as a watering hole for train workers at the nearby depot.

By the 1890s, owner Al Eustice began to rent the upstairs rooms to local residents and devised plans to upgrade the building. "By the late 1890s a barn roof was put on the building. It was the largest building in the community so it served as a hall for weddings and social events, and there was also a barber shop on the east end," Jim Herbert, current manager of the Glenview House, says. "In 1899, townspeople and others from the area met on the second floor to incorporate the town of Glenview." Later in the year, Eunice sold the building to John Dilg, who added a third story that was used as a dancehall. From that time on the bar was known as Dilg's.

A fire ravaged the dancehall 1922. This was during the era of Prohibition, but the bar and rooming house remained. "During Prohibition the place survived by selling near beer or home-made beer," Herbert says. "The owners lived in the back room, and there were rumors that the rooms above the bar were also rented out for 'other purposes.'"

The present owner bought the bar in 1988 and changed the name from Dilg's to the Glenview House. Looking at the worn wooden floors, the pressed tin ceilings, and the hand-painted signs on the windows, not much else has changed. More like a Chicago tavern, Glenview House caters to blue-collar workers and local residents. As the lively patrons carry pitchers of beer, laugh, and light an occasional outdoor cigar, you cannot help but look towards the railroad tracks and ponder. Even though the new buildings and strip malls have significantly altered the landscape, Glenview House still provides a place to blow off steam.

Glenview House has since been purchased by a new owner and is currently closed. In September 2010, the Glenview Village Board signed off on the new owner's renovation plans.

ALTHOUGH THE GLENVIEW HOUSE IS A hopping bar, a real grown-up venue, Glenview is most noted as a family-friendly city. Glenview's **Kohl Children's Museum** (2100 Patriot Blvd., 847/832-6600) draws families and school groups from all over the region. A hands-on museum for kids, some of its activities include a Habitat Park, children's library, discovery maze, car care, and pet vet. The museum is built with environmentally friendly materials and also features exhibits on solar energy, wind power, and conservation.

OLDEST GOLF COURSE— PUBLIC

DOWNERS GROVE PUBLIC GOLF COURSE
2420 Haddow Avenue
Downers Grove (1892)

In 1892, golf was little more than an obscure club sport, equivalent to bocce ball or cricket. Imported from Scotland, golf was seen as a hobby of the idle rich (see next entry). Players used iron and leather clubs and golf balls made from horsehide. In 1892, the Chicago Golf Club built a small course in what was then called Belmont, Illinois. Today, it is the oldest public golf course west of the Allegheny Mountains.

Charles Blair Macdonald designed the nine-hole course. Born in Niagara Falls, Ontario, but raised in Chicago, Macdonald fell in love with the game while he was a student at the University of St. Andrews. He was the first U.S. amateur champion and is known as "the father of golf architecture." He designed the National Golf Links of America in Southampton, New York, and the Mid-Ocean Club in Bermuda.

The original motivation to build the course, though, came from England's Sir Henry Wood. As Council General to the 1893 World's Fair, Wood helped create the Chicago Golf Club. In 1894, the Chicago Golf Club developed an 18-hole course in Wheaton. After adding a clubhouse (which burned down in 1924), the facility became known as the Belmont Golf Club. In 1930, the Slepicka family purchased the course and operated it as a private club. In 1968, the Downers Grove Park District bought the golf course for $750 and renamed it the Downers Grove Public Golf Course.

Nestled in a tree-lined area near a nature preserve, the course has four sets of tees and is challenging enough for skilled players to practice but simple enough for beginners to have fun. The complex also has a driving range with 24 hitting stations, a clubhouse with a snack bar, and an outdoor patio overlooking the golf course. The facility is open every day until ground snow.

LOVE NATURE AND EXERCISE, BUT CAN'T swing a club? Then why not head over to the **Morton Arboretum** (4100 Illinois Route 53, Lisle, 630/968-0074). The Morton Arboretum was founded in 1922 by Joy Morton (1855–1934), whose family founded the Morton Salt Company. The inspiration came from her father, J. Sterling Morton, who helped to originate the first Arbor Day in 1872. The Arboretum includes 4,117 different kinds of trees, shrubs, and other plants, represented by more than 182,000 specimens arranged according to five groups: taxonomic collections (e.g., elms and oaks), geographic collections (e.g., trees and shrubs from China), special habitats (e.g., plants of acid soils), horticultural collections, and collections of rare and endangered plants. Sprawled out over 1,700 acres, it is settled on a scenic valley created by the ice age (the Valparaiso Moraine) and is also bisected by the eastern branch of the Du Page River. The fall colors are, to say the least, astounding. The Arboretum is open 365 days a year, from 7 AM to 7 PM (during long daylight months), and from dawn 'til dusk during the winter.

OLDEST GOLF COURSE— PRIVATE

MIDLOTHIAN GOLF COURSE
5000 147th Street
Midlothian (1898)

With founding members like Montgomery Ward, John G. Shedd, and George R. Thorne (Montgomery Ward company president), the Midlothian Country Club follows in the tradition of the Augusta National Golf Club, Pebble Beach, and other exclusive private institutions that put the green into the "green fees." The club's early founders had so much clout they built the Midlothian and Blue Island Railway to connect the clubhouse to the Rock Island Railway at 147th Street.

Built on the Tinley Moraine, in what was then called Rexford Crossing, the area's rolling hills and natural valleys were lined with willow and oak trees. The golf course's and later the village's names were inspired by Sir Walter Scott's *The Heart of Midlothian.*

After the turn of the century, Ward, Shedd, and other members of Chicago'e elite moved to the northern suburbs, but still the club prospered. It hosted the U.S. Open in 1914, the Hagen Invitational in 1939, and the Western Open in 1969 and 1973. Today it is a private club, with green fees ranging from $50 to $80.

OVER 100 YEARS AGO, THE OLDEST PRIvate golf course, Midlothian Golf Course, was the playground of industrial giants like Montgomery Ward and John G. Shedd. At about the same time, Lithuanian immigrants, like the fictional hero of Upton Sinclair's, *The Jungle*, Jurgus Rudkis, were settling in the neighborhood of Bridgeport, working ten hours days and arriving soaked in blood and sawdust at bars like **Schaller's Pump** (see Oldest Bar, p. 69) for a drink before returning to their bungalows. It is a credit to the American system that today, the culture of Rudkis, represented by the **Balzekas Museum of Lithuanian Culture** (6500 S. Pulaski Rd., Chicago, 773/582-6500) is only a 10-mile drive from the golf course in Midlothian that the workers could only dream of seeing a century ago. Swords, costumes, and royal garb from the medieval period, as well as Roman coins found in Lithuania when it was overrun over 2,000 years ago, are just some of the artifacts you can find in this intimate museum. Collections of amber, the Lithuanian gem and good luck charm, plus exhibits on Chicago's Lithuanian community are also on display.

OLDEST ICE CREAM PARLOR

{ **PETERSEN'S RESTAURANT AND ICE CREAM PARLOUR**
1100 W. Chicago Avenue
Oak Park (1919) }

The year was 1919. Frank Lloyd Wright was working in his Oak Park studio, which is now a museum. A few blocks north, Ernest Hemingway had recently returned home from his stint as an ambulance driver during World War I and was nursing his physical and emotional wounds. Meanwhile, a Danish immigrant named Hans Petersen opened up an ice cream parlor on the quiet, quaint streets of suburban Oak Park on the western border of Chicago. It makes you wonder if Wright and Hemingway, two American icons, ever crossed paths, or even enjoyed a sundae at Petersen's on a warm summer day.

Nobody will ever know, but Chicagoland residents do know that Petersen's original ice cream recipe, which contains a whop-

ping 18 percent butterfat, has lasted for almost 90 years. During
the last nine decades it has survived competition from the take-
home, supermarket brands that emerged in the 1950s, ice cream
chains like Baskin-Robbins that grew during the 1970s, and the
ice milk and frozen yogurt eras of the 1980s and 1990s. The task
seems even more daunting when you realize that in 1919 there
were no refrigerators, freezers, or freezer trucks. Just making
ice cream was a chore in itself.

In 1846, Nancy Johnson invented the method of making ice
cream with a hand-cranked freezer, metal container, and salt.
In this process, ice and salt were packed in a large metal bucket,
lowering the freezing point of the ice. Milk was placed in the
inside bucket, and it froze when it came into contact with the
metal. The wooden paddle separated the ice milk from the cold
metal. But ice was needed not only for the ice cream itself, but
also to keep the ice cream cold once it was made. When Petersen opened his shop in 1919, ice had to be cut in giant chunks
from lakes and stored in ice houses insulated with straw for the
remainder of the season

In 1926, the first continuous process freezer for ice cream
was invented. This invention helped Petersen move his business to 1100 West Oak Park Avenue, just a half block away from
Wright's Home and Studio at 951 Chicago Avenue. Even though
it was the height of the Great Depression, Petersen's Restaurant
and Ice Cream Parlour was able to expand in 1931, adding food
items like hot dogs and sandwiches to the menu.

The post-war economic boom and emergence of the teenage hangout paved the way for further expansion. In 1950, Petersen's Restaurant and Ice Cream Parlour occupied the entire
building at 1100 Chicago Avenue, as the middle room became
the "Community Room" and the "School Room" on the north
end was added for parties. The Sweet Shoppe offered ice cream
cakes, pies, and candies for take out. Home refrigerators and

freezers opened up another market—hand-packed ice cream to take home. The aqua blue and orange containers soon became a familiar sight in local stores and supermarkets, with Petersen's preceding brands like Häagen-Dazs and Ben and Jerry's as the area's first gourmet ice cream. Petersen was so proud of his tradition, he gave the company to five loyal employees in 1963. In 1974, they sold the company to the Raniere family who ran it until February 2002.

Now, Daryl Bartelson and his family own Petersen's Restaurant and Ice Cream Parlour. Oak Park residents for over 22 years, the Bartelsons purchased the shop hoping to maintain an Oak Park tradition. They expanded the menu to include dinner specials and liquor. Unfortunately, changing tastes forced the Bartelsons to close the restaurant portion of the store in early 2007. Just as Chicagoans decried the closing of the original Berghoff in 2005, Oak Park families flocked to Petersen's to show their children the place where many generations enjoyed family outings. The ice cream store, still known as the Sweet Shoppe, has remained open. According to a representative of the Bartelson family, "The Sweet Shoppe will remain open so that people can still enjoy what Petersen's is most famous for: the ice cream. And it will remain open for a long time to come."

JUST THINK: THE MAN WHO MANY CON-
sider to be the nation's best known architect and the man who many consider to be our best known author had homes within a few blocks of each other in Oak Park. Completed in 1898, the **Frank Lloyd Wright Home and Studio** (951 Chicago Ave., 708/848-1976) features the design, gardens, kitchen, bedrooms, playrooms, and work area of Frank Lloyd Wright. Magnificently restored, the dark paneled wood, stained glass, and architectural details give visitors an intimate look into Wright's personal space and creative vision. It is only about two blocks from Petersen's Ice Cream Parlour. The **Ernest Hemingway Birthplace** (200 N. Oak Park Ave., 708/445-3071) is only a short drive from Wright's home/workspace and Petersen's. A sprawling Victorian mansion, this is where Hemingway lived for the early part of his life. You can see the kitchen where young Ernie ate, the backyard he played in, and artifacts including furniture, guns, and family photos. A 90-minute tour costs $7 and goes towards further preservation of the home.

OLDEST BALLROOM

 WILLOWBROOK BALLROOM
8900 W. Archer Avenue
Willow Springs (1921)

It is a warm Saturday night, and spring is in the air. A big band orchestra is playing "Sing, Sing, Sing" on a giant, maple dance floor. Dancers in zoot suits and gowns are jitterbugging and jumping to the Lindy Hop and Suzie Q. As a couple walks out into the parking lot, crickets chirp beneath the oak trees and the music drifts out into the moonlight. That sounds like a scene from a Frank Capra movie, but it's not. It's Willowbrook Ballroom.

The Willowbrook Ballroom started as a portable, wooden, outdoor dance floor before World War I. Back then it was called the Oh Henry Dance Hall. John Verderbar built the official dance hall in 1921 and there locals danced to the first sounds of jazz. In 1930, the pavilion burned to the ground, but people suffering through the Great Depression needed a place to let off steam, and on May 3, 1931, the Willowbrook Ballroom was rebuilt for $100,000 of Depression-era dollars.

The 1940s brought a flood of wartime energy flocking to the Oh Henry Dance Hall. An average of 10,000 people a week came to see local bands, and big name acts including Count Basie, Norm Crosby, Guy Lombardo, Glenn Miller, and Harry James. One of the most famous guests of the 1930s wasn't a musician at all. A girl named Mary was on her way home from the Oh Henry Dance Hall when she was struck by a car along Archer Avenue. To this day, ghost hunters make the journey from the Willowbrook Ballroom to Resurrection Cemetery (at 7200 Archer Road) in hopes of spotting "Resurrection Mary," the ghostly figure in a flowing white gown, making her way along Archer Avenue.

While the 1950s saw the decline of some big band ballrooms, the Oh Henry, renamed the Willowbrook Dance Hall in 1959, simply accommodated the times. Local Chicago bands, such as the Buckinghams and the Cryin' Shames, and national acts, like Chubby Checker, graced the stage during the swinging 1960s. With the 1970s came the onset of the disco era, and the Willowbrook once again evolved with the times. On weeknights, the room turned into a disco, and on weekends, acts like the Village People hustled across the stage.

Today, the room has almost come full circle, as big-name big bands like the Glenn Miller Orchestra grace the stage. The ballroom has also benefited from the popularity of country, swing, and salsa dancing, as the ballroom offers a space to dance as well as a chance to take dance lessons on Monday, Tuesday, and Wednesday nights. The best bet: go to the Dell Rhea Chicken Basket (see p. 225) for an early dinner, then check out the Willowbrook Ballroom on a Saturday night.

☞ EVERYBODY KNOWS ABOUT THE WILLOW-
brook Ballroom and Resurrection Mary. Her ghost and legend live on just three miles northeast of here in **Resurrection Cemetery** (7200 W. Archer Ave., Justice, IL), actually rated as one of the top cemeteries in the nation. It is not unusual to see deer munching silently on neatly mowed grass and wandering among the tombstones and mature trees on Resurrection's sprawling, beautiful grounds. Despite the pastoral setting, the cemetery will never outlive its reputation as the home of Resurrection Mary, one of the country's most famous ghosts. The bars to the cemetery's gate were said to have been bent by Mary's spirit in 1976 (who knew a wraith needed extra space to squeeze in and out of cemetery bars?). Cemetery officials say that it was a wayward truck that hit the steel bars and disfigured them, but photos taken at the time do indicate more of a melting/slow bending than they do a forced impact. Curious! After a view of the cemetery, the gates, and the Willowbrook Ballroom, visitors can drive a few miles west of the ballroom, to Kingery Road, and have a fried chicken dinner at the **Dell Rhea Chicken Basket** (see Oldest Route 66 Roadhouse, p. 225).

OLDEST DINER

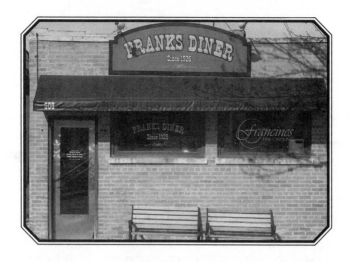

 FRANKS DINER
508 W. 58th Street
Kenosha, Wisconsin (1926)

I t is early morning at Franks Diner in Kenosha, Wisconsin. Co-owner Chris Schwartz takes two eggs in one hand. Cracking them in one motion, she pours them over the griddle sunny side up. The eggs sizzle alongside all the ingredients for a Garbage Plate: four giant hash brown patties, a cheeseburger, an order of Canadian bacon, a steak, three giant pancakes, and four piles of green pepper, onion, chopped ham, and hot peppers. Moving back and fourth behind her in an area two feet wide, her partner, Lynn Groleau, takes orders, clears and wipes the counters, makes coffee, pours juice, butters homemade toast, answers the phone, and shoves the bread in and out of a tiny toaster oven. Lynn and Chris perform this routine from six in the morning to two in the afternoon, six days a week.

Diners as shown in films and television shows usually refer to any inexpensive place that serves meat loaf, mashed potatoes, eggs and bacon, and black coffee at a counter. Most greasy spoons are not actually diners. A real diner is a railroad dining car that was abandoned by the decline of the railroads and growth of highways in the late 1920s and turned into a restaurant. Often equipped with gas and water hookups, griddles, and tables and chairs, many entrepreneurs bought and refitted the cars for little or nothing. Catering to truck drivers and factory workers who needed fast, inexpensive food between shifts, diner owners created thriving businesses with low start-up costs. They also created some enduring Americana.

In 1926, Anthony Franks had six horses pull a dining car to 266 West 58th Street. The dining car was built by the Jerry O'Mahoney firm in New Jersey. Anthony Franks learned of the opportunity through a magazine article and paid $7,500 for the car plus $325 in shipping charges. "The Franks Family operated the diner until 2001, when Lynn, myself, and a third partner named Kris Derwae bought the place," Schwartz says. "During the 1930s, 1940s, and into the 1950s and 1960s you had a large pool of diner-friendly workers to draw customers from. There were the Nash, Chrysler, and later the American Motors Auto Plants in Kenosha, as well as a Simmons Mattress, American Brass, and Snap-On-Tools factories, so the diner sometimes ran 24 hours a day."

Twenty feet wide by sixty feet long, with dark wooden paneling, antique ceiling fans, and a cast iron stove, Franks would be a ready-made set for any Roaring Twenties or Great Depression–era film. While the designers for Chicago-shot films like *The Road to Perdition* have overlooked this gem, the diner has been host to a unique list of entertainment luminaries, includ-

ing Duke Ellington, Bela Lugosi, the Three Stooges, and Lawrence Welk. "Back then a lot of tourists came here to enjoy the
Lake Michigan beaches and restaurants, and because of this
there was also an active entertainment scene," Groleau says.
"We had the Kenosha Theater and The Eagles Ballroom. We
are also happy to say that Kenosha is coming back."

A new trolley line, lakefront condos, multi-million dollar Civil War and history museums, and a new string of restaurants
have been the keys to revitalizing Kenosha. Accessible by Metra
train from Chicago, a stop at Franks would be a perfect beginning for a day trip north of the border. Although the city has
made enormous efforts to transform itself, the smaller, personal
efforts, like those of Grouleau and Schwartz, have also made a
difference in the town.

"When we bought this place the business was pretty deplet-
ed," Schwartz says. "We put a lot of work into it, cold, early
mornings in front of the grill and late nights spent talking about
how to manage the place, but it has paid off."

Grouleau and Schwartz have not only built up the business,
but developed a new menu with over one hundred items. Most
of them are diner standards like bacon and eggs, patty melts,
tuna melts, chili, biscuits and gravy, turkey clubs, malts, shakes,
and grilled cheese. There are also items unique to Franks, like
the French toast on homemade bread, the half-pound Bleu Schu
Burger, the Bates Burger, the Spam Sandwich, and the Garbage
Plate.

But the most distinctive thing about Franks is its history. As
you sit at the counter, you can imagine men in fedoras talking
about Babe Ruth or President Roosevelt. And while pop artists have made a fortune selling versions of Edward Hopper's
Nighthawks featuring Marilyn Monroe, Elvis Presley, and James
Dean, a "Nighthawks," featuring Lugosi, Ellington, Welk, and
the Three Stooges at Franks, would be a work of art indeed.

DECADES OF CHEESE AND BRATWURST jokes from "hip" Chicagoans aside, a drive to Kenosha just might be the best day trip from Chicago. Only a 90-minute drive from Chicago's Loop, you can hit Franks Diner for a giant breakfast, then see Kenosha's collection of small but fascinating museums. The newest and coolest is the **Kenosha Civil War Museum** (5400 1st Ave., 262/653-4141). Opened in June 2008, it is the multi-million dollar permanent home of the Palumbo Collection, which contains over 5,000 flags, swords, badges, books, and other Civil War artifacts. The **Kenosha Public Museum** (5500 1st Ave., 262/653-4140) is a quaint museum, which will likely remind Chicagoans of the Academy of Sciences Museum in Lincoln Park. Its largest exhibits include dinosaur bones and excavations of mammoth elephants, wolves, and other relics from the ice age. The **Kenosha History Center** (220 51st Pl., 262/654-5770), located on St. Simmons Island under the lighthouse, is also within walking distance of the Kenosha Public and Civil War museums. One of several things that makes the history center better than many small town museums is its exhibit of almost a dozen cars from the American Motors Plant, which was formerly located in Kenosha. Remember the Gremlin, Javelin, and The Pacer? You can find them here. The town of Kenosha also offers a rolling replica of a 1930s streetcar that you can ride around town for a quarter. Hungry for lunch or dinner? There are plenty of bars and restaurants along 6th Avenue, once again, a very short walk from the museums.

OLDEST ROUTE 66 ROADHOUSE

DELL RHEA CHICKEN BASKET
65 Joliet Road, just off I-55 and Route 83
Willowbrook (1928)

Route 66 is now a part of American folklore. It has its own PBS documentaries, books, calendars, clubs, festivals, and even a 1960s television series. Established in the late 1920s, the Dell Rhea Chicken Basket, with its glowing neon sign, fried chicken, catfish, and mashed potatoes, almost seems like it emerged from the verses of Route 66's most famous tribute, the Bobby Troup song "(Get Your Kicks On) Route 66."

According to Patrick Rhea, son of longtime owner Dell Rhea, "The place really started in the late 1960s when Route 66 was commissioned. It was originally a gas station located on the property next door." Rhea, who tends bar at the Chicken Basket, stands up and walks past a neon rooster and several walls full of Route 66 memorabilia which decorate the restaurant.

"It was about 500 feet from here," Rhea says, pointing out the window. "There were two repair bays, and a counter and two booths that served pop, pie, and cold sandwiches for the people who were waiting to get their cars done. The owner really didn't like changing oil all day, and as the highway became more popular, two local women suggested that he cook fried chicken. They made him a deal—if he bought all the eggs and chickens from their farm, they would give him the recipe and cook the chicken for free."

Have you ever eaten a fast food hamburger an hour after it has been made? Have you tasted—God forbid—a cold hot dog? Fried chicken is one of the few fast foods that tastes almost as good cold as it does hot. Keep it out of the sun, and the chicken will stay good for a couple of days. So if a family bought a basket of lightly breaded, crispy fried chicken on a Monday morning at Dell Rhea Chicken Basket, it would probably still be tasty when they hit Colorado.

"As Route 66 continued to grow, so did the restaurant," Rhea says. "This building opened in 1946, when the highway was in full swing." The restaurant grew so popular that it became a bus stop and depot for drivers and passengers who bought their ticket and a basket of fried chicken at the same stop. During spring, summer, and autumn the restaurant filled with motoring travelers, the road trip business slowed during Chicago's cold winter months. In order to attract business the owner came up with another gimmick: "During the 1940s and 1950s there was ice skating on the roof. The building was built with steel tresses and there was a parapet with a spotlight and sill cocks that gushed out water. So the owner would flood the roof and hire professional skaters to put on a show. People driving along the road would see it and stop in for some chicken."

The restaurant thrived until Route 66 closed in 1960. Then, like so many great motels, diners, gift shops, and bars that sprung up along the road, the Chicken Basket struggled. In 1963, Dell (short for Delbert) Rhea decided to give the business a go. "My father took over the restaurant in 1963," Patrick Rhea says. "He was the longtime owner of the Woodbine (now the Kerry Piper) Restaurant down the street, and was a very well-known guy involved in politics, and was also the director of the Chicago Convention Bureau at the Stevens Hotel. So when he put his name up on the sign, the rest was history."

After the death of his father, Patrick Rhea took over the business. A strong supporter of tradition, he tried to keep everything the same, although the glowing orange and blue neon sign that reads "Dell Rhea Chicken Basket/Cocktail Lounge" almost didn't survive. It seems that some of the old connotations associated with neon like "neon jungle" and "the light of sin" were heard within the village of Willowbrook. In 1979, the village filed suit against Rhea and his neon sign, trying to force him to take it down. "We received a letter saying that there was a village ordinance against free-standing signs," Rhea remembers. "We had to hire lawyers and get other local business owners to fight the village. It took over ten years, from 1979 until the early 1990s, to keep the right to have our sign."

In many ways, getting rid of the neon sign would have been easier. "Neon signs, with their many thin tubes, are continually exposed to weather, vandalism, and even a pebble that could ricochet off the road," Rhea explains. "It is very hard and expensive, since you need a qualified person, to repair them. It is even more expensive to build them from scratch. A new neon sign would probably cost about $50,000, while a plastic-faced sign [McDonald's, Burger King, and Dunkin Donuts] with their dull, fluorescent bulbs, would probably cost about $10,000. But as far as we are concerned, it is a classic part of the restaurant, and I would do whatever it takes for it to remain this way."

It seems that Rhea's efforts paid off. In May 2006, the Illinois Historic Preservation Agency made the Chicken Basket a state landmark. Why? Because it is a special piece of America. It's about a half-hour drive from Chicago, and the fried chicken is still made from the original recipe that the farmers' wives came up with in 1928. In true roadhouse tradition, the restaurant and bar also features blues and country bands, and events like Frank Sinatra or Dean Martin tributes on weekends. The Chicken Basket even hosts antique car and motorcycle shows

"A lot of people want to buy me out, or buy part of the name and turn this into a franchise," Rhea says. "I guess now people can't afford to pay the fees for a name like McDonald's, but they still want to have a known name before they open. This isn't a franchise..."

ROUTE 66 HAS UNFORTUNATELY CLOSED down long ago. Dell Rhea's, just off Illinois Route 55, is one of the lone local survivors as far as bars, juke joints, and diners along the famed Mother Road. This stretch of I-55 (the Stevenson Expressway in Chicagoland) parallels the **Illinois and Michigan Canal**. Built in the 1840s and '50s by hundreds of Irish and other immigrants, many of whom perished while doing so, the canal was a vital link between Chicago and eventually the Mississippi River. The trailhead for the I&M Canal is located at **Channahon State Park** (25302 W. Story St., Channahon, 815/467-4271). It is also the start of the **I&M Canal Bike Trail**. Perhaps the best bike path in all of Northern Illinois, the I&M trail is a crushed limestone path that runs from Channahon to **Starved Rock State Park** (south side of the Illinois River between Utica and LaSalle-Peru, 815/667-4726). Pedaling from Channahon, you ride parallel to both the Des Planes River and the I&M Canal. Along the way you'll pass antique barns, farms, and several 1850s limestone locks and dams used for the canal. By the way, most of the path is covered by a canopy of trees, and the fall colors may be the best this side of New Hampshire. To get there, take I-55 south to exit 248 Route 6 and turn right on Route 6 going west for 2.5 miles. Turn left on South Fryer Street, going south for .04 miles, then turn right on West Story Street to the park. After a hard day's riding, feast on Dell Rhea's fried chicken and kick back with a cold one.

 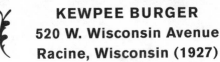

KEWPEE BURGER
520 W. Wisconsin Avenue
Racine, Wisconsin (1927)

The wax paper on their burgers displays a giant, naked Kewpee doll and reads "hamburg-pickle-on-top makes your heart go flippity-flop." For those of you who aren't burger historians, the word Hamburg refers to the city of Hamburg, Germany, where hamburgers were invented. Kewpee Burger is a throw back to the days before "burger" was a household term; Kewpee Burgers uses "hamburgs" instead.

If that doesn't give you a clue to the 1927 origins of the Racine Kewpee Burger, then the building definitely will. Composed of pink granite walls, a black granite foundation, and narrow slit windows with faux stainless steel edging, Kewpie Burger is an Art Deco oasis in what is otherwise the picture of medium-sized town America that Racine, Wisconsin, is.

The Racine Kewpee Burger is one of the few remaining lo-
cations of one of the earliest hamburger chains. White Castle
was the nation's first hamburger chain, established in 1921, but
Kewpee Burger wasn't far behind—it originated in 1926. The
Kewpee chain had over 200 restaurants east of the Mississippi
River before World War II. The stores in the chain were primarily located in medium-sized, semi-industrial towns like Grand
Rapids and Kalamazoo in Michigan, or South Bend and Mun-
cie in Indiana. Some claim that Wendy's restaurant founder and
Ohio native Dave Thomas got the idea for Wendy's after eating
at Kewpee—both are based in Lima, Ohio. Today, there are only
six Kewpee Burgers left. Along with the one in Racine, there are
three restaurants in Lima, and two in Lansing, Michigan.

Dick Stanford and Allen Durkee opened the Racine Kewpee
in 1927. It began as a basic garage-looking building with small
windows and tin smokestacks poking through the roofs. The
town was home to many factories, and workers streamed in
from seven in the morning through eleven at night and later.
Because the burgers were only five cents, Kewpee did not suffer
as much as other businesses during the Great Depression.

As the economy improved in 1939, the building was remodeled and given a white, Art Deco diner look. Now owned by
Durkee and Walter Block, it cruised through the fabulous 1950s,
and was able to stave off challenges from the mega-chains like
McDonald's and Burger King through the 1960s and 1970s.

One of the reasons Kewpee Burger endures is the quality
of the food. Unlike the newer chains, which serve machine-
formed, frozen patties, Kewpee's burgers come into the restaurant as fresh red meat. The hamburgs are formed into squares
and patted down once they hit the grill. The result is not only a
tasty burger, but one with a somewhat loose texture that combines the flavors of mom's hand-packed "flying saucers" with
that hard to copy fast-food taste—is it the grease? The fish sand-

wiches also have a unique flavor, similar to what you would taste at a Lenten fish fry. The fact that each food item seems to be at least a bit different is not the only thing that makes Kewpee Burger a special hybrid between a chain restaurant and a traditional diner—there's also the homemade chili and hand-dipped ice cream sundaes, shakes, and malts. While most fast food chain customers order their food and bring it back to the table in paper wrappers, waiters deliver the food on real, diner-style plates. The homemade root beer is a real treat, and the server will pour you free refills.

Kewpee has not only had to fight off competition from the fast-food giants to survive for 80-plus years. In 1962 a Racine City parking lot was built over Kewpee. Even with cars streaming overhead, Kewpee never had to close. Finally, in 1995 it was determined that the ramp was no longer safe and had to be demolished.

According to owner Dave Kristopeit, "The city of Racine acquired the Kewpee under the right of eminent domain and agreed to help in relocation as required under Wisconsin law. Because no adequate replacement property could be found, I decided to buy the old property back from the city after the demolition and rebuilt it on the same site it had been on for 70 years."

The new Kewpee was built in 1997, and the interior is as interesting as the outside. The restaurant has two U-shaped counters with stools that are set about two and a half feet above the tile floor. The walls are lined with kewpee dolls and kewpee memorabilia, including a glass case with over 50 new and antique Kewpee dolls, Kewpee watches, Kewpee key chains, photos, and sweatshirts. This might be the only distraction from what is otherwise a cool half-day trip worth the 90-minute drive from Chicago: As you eat, you are surrounded by Kewpee dolls. With a shock of Mohawk-style hair and a little curlycue dip in front, they are often dressed in antique clothes and their hard, plastic eyes stare at you like a combination voodoo doll and Chucky doll. It makes you wonder if they can get up and walk around at night.

DAY TRIP! FEW CHICAGOANS SEE RACINE, Wisconsin, as a destination, but Kewpee Burger can be just one stop on a Racine mini-excursion. Other points of interest include the **Wind Point Lighthouse** (4725 Lighthouse Dr., 262/639-3777) on Highway 22 and Christopher Columbus Causeway. Built in 1890, the 108-foot tall beacon was built for traffic on the Great Lakes, but looks like any classic lighthouse you'd find on the Maine or Oregon coast. At 50 acres, Racine's **North Beach** (Michigan Blvd. & Kewaunee St., 262/636-9131) is one of the largest public urban beaches along Lake Michigan, and has something of a "West Coast" feel. You might also want to drop by the **S.C. Johnson Administration Building** (1525 Howe St.), the largest commercial structure designed by Frank Lloyd Wright's firm.

 TIVOLI THEATER
5021 Highland Avenue
Downers Grove (1928)

With gold leaf fountains, terra cotta ornamentation, red carpets, and ceilings that seemed to stretch to the sky, great movie palaces such the Granada and the Uptown gave the average person the chance to visit Egyptian thrones, Oriental gardens, and French palaces for as little as a nickel. The onset of television and the urban renewal of the 1960s sounded the death knell for the great majority of these celluloid kingdoms. The Granada was turned into a senior citizens home. The Century was made into a shopping mall. Some, like the Uptown, sit idly, waiting for refurbishment that may never come. Others, such as the Chicago, the Oriental, and Joliet's Rialto, became venues for live entertainment.

The relatively new suburb of Downers Grove holds the oldest movie theater. Located at the corner of Warren and Highland avenues, the Tivoli Theater opened on Christmas Day, 1928, to a crowd of 4,000 people. Designed by Van Guten and Van Guten for the Balaban and Katz chain, the theater was one of the first in the country to be built especially for "talkies." The outside of the theater contains spiraling terra cotta, two-story French windows, and a glowing marquee. The interior was fashioned in the style of the French Renaissance, with red, gold, and blue dominating the color scheme. The theater had 1,390 seats, all made of red and gold horsehair, and the lobbies and lounges required over 1,500 yards of red carpeting.

Like most movie palaces, the theater was an escape during the Great Depression and the site of patriotic movies, news-reels, and stage shows during World War II. Many of Chicago's great theaters suffered from competition with television, but the Tivoli was buoyed by a new population of baby boomers who had migrated to the suburbs.

In 1976, Willis Johnson purchased the property, and dedicated himself to refurbishing the theater in response to the competition from the new shopping center multiplexes. In 1996, the theater was repainted using special gold leaf paint, which cost up to $100 a gallon. While a changing economy destroyed many old movie palaces, the residents of Downers Grove and other nearby communities rallied to raise funds for restoring the building. Renovations completed in 2003 included 824 yards of new carpeting, new seats, and modernized restrooms. In 2006, the sound system was replaced, and the theater now boasts the acoustic power of ten symphony orchestras.

The Tivoli shows first-run, blockbuster films but it is also a center for arts and culture in Downers Grove. The Midwest Bal-let Theater and the West Town Chorus perform at the venue, and the Village of Downers Grove's annual summer celebration is held there the first week of June. The After Hours Film Society also screens classic, art, and foreign films at the theater on the second and fourth Mondays of each month.

👉 WHILE DOWNERS GROVE HAS A NUMBER of new shops and restaurants, visitors who want to keep a Roaring 20s feel to their day can drive a few miles to **Cantigny Park** (1 S. 151 Winfield Rd., Wheaton, 630/668-5161) for 500 acres of nature, museums, activities, and events. The former home of Col. Robert McCormick, longtime publisher of the *Chicago Tribune* (see Oldest Newspaper, p. 18), Cantigny's sprawling grounds and grand buildings are suitable for Jay Gatsby. Instead of romance, however, the estate and its two museums are dedicated to the military, primarily the First Division, also known as The Big Red One. The park land includes dozens of tanks, cannons, and military vehicles from World War I (when McCormick served) up through today. The Cantigny museums contain over 10,000 artifacts including medals, posters, weapons, and flags. They also host lectures, car shows, military re-enactments, author signings, and concerts. If you are not into military history, the formal gardens, which include a rose garden and the 35-room mansion brimming with antiques and paintings are, once again, Gatsby-worthy.

OLDEST BARBECUE

 RUSSELL'S BARBECUE
1621 N. Thatcher Avenue
Elmwood Park (1930)

It is a warm summer night, and the smell of barbecued meat drifts up a 75-year-old smokestack, wafting across the road through a stand of thick oak woods and down to the edge of the riverbank. Cars sit in the parking lot under the glow of a wraparound neon sign that reads "Beef, Chicken, Ham—RUSSEL'S BARBECUE—Pork, Ribs, Drinks." Above, a swinging white shingle sign practically shouts out, "Coca Cola" in bright red letters over a picture of a thick, green glass bottle.

If this sounds like a passage from a novel set in Georgia or Alabama you may be right, but in this book it describes the scene from Russell's Barbecue. When it was built, the area bounded on the west by the Cook County Forest Preserves and the Des

Plaines River was little more than a backwoods holler. Seventy-five years later the area around Thatcher Avenue just west of the Chicago city limits is still relatively quiet and out of the way. But for longtime area residents, Russell's is no secret.

Russell's Barbecue started only a few short months after the stock market crash of October 1929. The country had just entered the Great Depression, and the suburb of Elmwood Park was no different. While many downtown steakhouses suffered, the sliced pork-on-a-roll with a side of beans at Russell's Barbecue was inexpensive enough for even Depression-era families. The end of World War II turned the area from a slightly populated riverfront to booming suburbia. Russell's Barbeque expanded, and the advent of the automobile made the restaurant a family destination.

The restaurant has changed little since the 1950s. The tables and booths are ranch-style solid wood seats and benches. The restaurant offers indoor dining, a semi-open patio, and an outdoor picnic area. Many of Chicago's barbecues are derived from the Mississippi and Alabama traditions of wood-smoked meats dry-rubbed then basted with a thick, spicy sauce, but the pork sandwiches, barbecue ribs, and beef brisket at Russell's Barbeque are cooked in an oven with small amounts of milder sauce. The meat is generally leaner than what you find at most barbeque joints. Their motto: "We search everywhere for the leanest, highest quality meats available. The results are tender, mouth watering ribs and pork sandwiches."

LOCATED ON THE OUTSKIRTS OF CHICAGO, Russell's Barbecue is only a half-mile west of the **Balmoral Race Track** (26435 S. Dixie Hwy., 708/672-1414). Russell's is nestled on the edge of the Des Plaines River, with the entrance to the barbecue about 20 yards from the shore. While it does not provide the scenic vistas of rivers in northern Wisconsin or Michigan's UP, the **Des Plaines River** can give local canoeists and kayakers a place to stretch their arms and get a breath of fresh air. The best place to launch a personal watercraft is at Irving Park and River roads, about two miles north. Just park your car in the large lot; it's only a 20-yard portage down a gradual slope with limestone walls and a gravel path to the landing. Entering and exiting your craft will be as water- and mud-free as you can get. Once on the river, bordered by the Cook County Forest Preserves on either side, do not be surprised if you see deer, great blue herons, muskrats, and other wildlife. The deer are especially tame—they often stare at you! Russell's Barbecue is about 2.5 miles downstream. Paddle, or just float, depending on the current. You can get out of the water at North Avenue, about 30 yards from Russell's. By the time you're here, you will have worked up an appetite for ribs, chicken, and other barbecue (the energy you'll need for the trip back).

OLDEST DRIVE-IN MOVIE THEATER

CASCADE DRIVE-IN
1100 E. North Avenue
West Chicago (1952)

orget rock and roll, high school football, and the family vacation in a station wagon—nothing symbolizes the glory days of post-war America more than the drive-in movie. The process was invented by Richard Hollingshead, who nailed a screen to a tree and projected a movie onto it in his driveway in Camden, New Jersey. In 1933, he opened the first drive-in movie theater. The first drive-ins had to overcome problems with sound, which were solved by placing speakers on posts with underground wires. Early owners of drive-ins also had to deal with lines of cars blocking each other and invasions of bugs attracted to the lights. But suburban sprawl and the availability of automobiles to teenagers in the 1950s made the drive-in part of the American landscape. According to www. driveintheater.com, there were 95 drive-ins across America in

1942. By 1958, there were 5,000. The largest drive-in theater in patron capacity was the All-Weather Drive-In of Copiague, New York. All-Weather had parking space for 2,500 cars, an indoor 1,200-seat viewing area, a kid's playground, a full service restaurant, and a shuttle train that took customers from their cars and around the 28-acre theater lot.

The Cascade Drive-in opened in 1952 during the peak of the drive-in era. It is the largest outdoor cinema in Illinois, with a capacity for 1,200 cars. The concession stand sells popcorn, hot dogs, burgers, ice cream, and other treats. For those of you who grew up in the city proper or haven't gone to a drive-in, it is a festive event akin to going to an open-air rock concert or fireworks display, and an experience that shouldn't be missed.

Movie goers arrive early, usually in large groups or families who arrive by van or RV. They quickly spread out lawn chairs, picnic blankets, small grills, and tiki torches. While 1950s and '60s music plays over the large speaker system, children throw Frisbees, footballs, and softballs, dogs roam (pets are allowed), and adults sip on beers. Drive-ins are infamous for late-night necking sessions: teenagers and young couples hold hands, waiting eagerly for the cover of darkness. Soon, the sun sets and the moon starts to rise over the horizon. Sound arrives via the classic, pole-mounted speaker that can also be placed on a dashboard, or by tuning in to 88.5 FM on a car radio. As the grey of twilight descends over the theater, retro ads with boys in crew cuts and "mom and sis" urge patrons to visit the concession stands. Then come the previews, and as complete darkness falls over the area, the feature film begins.

The drive-in is probably not the place to see the latest film touted for an Academy Award. On the other hand, if you are in the mood for a cartoon feature, comedy, or horror offering, there is probably no better way to see it than at a drive-in on a warm summer's night.

In recent years, Chicagoland has seen a number of drive-ins go dark. These include The Hi-Lite 30 Drive-In (Aurora), The

Bel-Air Drive-In (3101 South Cicero Avenue in Cicero), and the McHenry Indoor/Outdoor Theater (1510 North Chapel Hill Road in McHenry). The Cascade Drive-In is thriving—on some weekend nights cars lining up on North Avenue are actually turned away. The Cascade Drive-In shows the latest releases, usually double features, seven nights a week April through September. Starting times vary with the time of the sunset. More information can be found at cascadedrivein.com or by calling 630/231-3150.

WHILE THE CASCADE DRIVE-IN IS LOCATED on a somewhat isolated stretch of North Avenue (Highway 64), it is only a few miles east of St. Charles. Perfect for a day trip, **St. Charles** was formerly a getaway and resort town for wealthy Chicagoans during the 1920s. The highlight of the city is the **Hotel Baker** (100 W. Main St., 630/584-2100). Built on the banks of the **Fox River** just above a dam, the hotel was replete with luxury amenities when built in 1928. Unfortunately, the Great Depression hit two years later. The hotel was lovingly restored recently, and the lounge attached to its **Rox City Grill** restaurant (630/845-5800) often features '20s-era blues and jazz, Thursday through Saturday. Across the street is the **Arcadia Theater** (105 E. Main St., 630/587-8400). Built in 1926 with 1,009 seats, it is a 1920s movie palace worthy of the great Chicago theaters. It has also been restored to its original splendor and features acts ranging from KC and the Sunshine Band to Martin Short, America, the Guess Who, and Sly and the Family Stone. May through October, visitors can get another dose of nostalgia on the **St. Charles Paddlewheel River Boat** (2 North Ave., 630/584-2334), which cruises the Fox River near **Pottawatomie Park** (1/2-mile north of Main St. on North 2nd Ave., 630/584-1885).

OLDEST CHICAGO— PHOTO CREDITS

p. 2   Photo by author David Anthony Witter.

p. 6   Photo by author David Anthony Witter.

p. 11   Photo by author David Anthony Witter.

p. 15   Photo by author David Anthony Witter.

p. 18   Photo by author David Anthony Witter.

p. 20   Photo by author David Anthony Witter.

p. 24   Photo by author David Anthony Witter.

p. 27   Photo by author David Anthony Witter.

p. 30   Photo by author David Anthony Witter.

p. 32   Photo by author David Anthony Witter.

p. 35   Photo by author David Anthony Witter.

p. 39   Photo by author David Anthony Witter.

p. 42   Photo by author David Anthony Witter.

p. 46   Photo courtesy of St. Ignatius College Prep.

p. 50   Photo by author David Anthony Witter.

p. 54   Photo by author David Anthony Witter.

p. 59   Photo by author David Anthony Witter.

p. 62   Photo by author David Anthony Witter.

p. 65   Photo courtesy of Merz Apothecary.

p. 69   Photo by author David Anthony Witter.

p. 74   Photo by author David Anthony Witter.

p. 76   Photo by author David Anthony Witter.

p. 81   Photo by author David Anthony Witter.

p. 87   Photo by author David Anthony Witter.

p. 90   Photo by author David Anthony Witter.

p. 93   Photo courtesy of Central Camera.

p. 98   Photo by author David Anthony Witter.

p. 102 Photo by author David Anthony Witter.

p. 106 Photo by author David Anthony Witter.

p. 109 Photo by author David Anthony Witter.

p. 112 Photo by author David Anthony Witter.

p. 115 Photo by author David Anthony Witter.

p. 120   Photo by author David
          Anthony Witter.

p. 123   Photo by author David
          Anthony Witter.

p. 127   Photo by author David
          Anthony Witter.

p. 129   Photo by author David
          Anthony Witter.

p. 133   Photo by author David
          Anthony Witter.

p. 136   Photo by author David
          Anthony Witter.

p. 140   Photo by author David
          Anthony Witter.

p. 144   Photo by author David
          Anthony Witter.

p. 147   Photo by author David
          Anthony Witter.

p. 154   Photo by author David
          Anthony Witter.

p. 157   Photo courtesy of Italian
          Village.

p. 163   Photo by author David
          Anthony Witter.

p. 171   Photo by Chris Costanzo.

p. 174   Photo by author David
          Anthony Witter.

p. 176   Photo by author David
          Anthony Witter.

p. 182   Photo by Chris Costanzo.

p. 184   Photo by author David
          Anthony Witter.

p. 188   Photo by author David
          Anthony Witter.

p. 193   Photo courtesy of Susie
          Castro.

p. 194   Photo courtesy of Susie
          Castro.

p. 196   Photo by author David
          Anthony Witter.

p. 200   Photo courtesy of Delmark
          Records.

p. 206   Photo by author David
          Anthony Witter.

p. 209   Photo courtesy of Downers
          Grove Park District.

p. 212   Photo courtesy of Midlo-
          thian Country Club.

p. 214   Phoo by author David
          Anthony Witter.

p. 218   Photo by author David
          Anthony Witter.

p. 221   Photo by author David
          Anthony Witter.

p. 225   Photo by author David
          Anthony Witter.

p. 230   Photo courtesy of Classic
          Cinemas.

p. 233   Photo by author David
          Anthony Witter.

p. 237   Photo by author David
          Anthony Witter.

p. 240   Photo by author David
          Anthony Witter.

Spot illustrations from Dover Publications.

ACKNOWLEDGMENTS

I did not want *Oldest Chicago* to be a guidebook of lists, but a series of small stories and articles. For this reason I wanted to gather most of the information from firsthand sources in the hope of providing a more personal perspective on each establishment, its history, and its place in Chicago lore. A majority of the information for this book was gathered from personal interviews with the current owners or descendants of the original owners (oftentimes both) as well as historians, company presidents, communications officers, and employees of the various businesses or institutions. These include:

Maurice Berman (Superdawg), Richard Brown (Newberry Library), Alfredo Capitanini (Italian Village), Alex Castro (La Guadalupana), John Chandler (St. Ignatius), Franco Chiappetti

(Chiappetti Lamb and Veal), Joe Colucci (Division Street Russian Baths), Chris Donovan (House of Glunz), George Filbert (Filbert's), Albert Flesch (Central Camera), Jim Herbert (Glenview House), Doug Jaeger (Jaeger Funeral Home), Roy Larsen (First United Methodist Church), Bob Koester (Jazz Record Mart), Edward Levi (Iwan Ries and Co.), Edward Maldonado (Clarke House), Tom Munley (McInerney Funeral Home), Abdul Qaiyum (Merz Apothecary), Jean Paspalas (Athenian Candle), Delores Reynolds (Army and Lou's), Patrick Rhea (Dell Rhea's Chicken Basket), John Roeser III (Roeser's Bakery), Dan Sampson (Noble Horse), Chris Schwartz (House of Glunz), and Dean Walter (C.D. Peacock Jewelers).

I also used the following books to either supplement the material in interviews or to provide second-hand information on locations where a spokesperson was unavailable.

Berkow, Ira. *Maxwell Street: Survival in a Bazaar.* New York: Doubleday and Company, 1977.

Cowdery, Chuck, "Maxwell Street, Still Hanging On" (Maxwell Street Coalition Paper, Chicago, 1997).

Grossman, James R., Ann Durkin Keating, Janice L. Reiff , eds. *The Encyclopedia of Chicago.* Chicago: University of Chicago Press, 2004.

Heisler, Raymond, *St. Ignatius College Prep: 125 Years of Jesuit Education.* Chicago: St. Ignatius College Prep, 1994.

Larsen, Roy and Mary Johnson. *Born in A Log Cabin, Alive at 175.* Chicago: The First United Methodist Church, 2007.

Hucke, Matt and Ursula Bielski. *Graveyards of Chicago: The People, History, Art, and Lore of Cook County Cemeteries.* Chicago: Lake Claremont Press, 1999.

In areas where neither firsthand information nor printed material were available, the following web sites were used:

- ⇨ www.classiccinemas.com

- ⇨ www.musicboxtheater.com

- ⇨ www.olstpats.org

- ⇨ www.pbs.org/blackpress/news_bios/defender.html

- ⇨ www.scubachicago.com

- ⇨ www.greenmilljazz.com

INDEX

ABOUT THE AUTHOR

avid Anthony Witter grew up in Lincoln Park in the 1970s, and watched as the community changed completely in less than a decade. He attended Alcott Grammar School and Lane Technical High School, received a B.A. in Writing from Columbia College, and earned a B.A. in Secondary Education from Northeastern Illinois University. A teacher of Special Education and English, he has worked for the Chicago Public Schools for 16 years. He currently teaches at Chicago's Kelly High School. A freelance writer and photographer, he is a regular contributor to *New City* and *Fra Noi*. His work has also appeared in the *Washington Post, Chicago Tribune, Chicago Reader, Living Blues, Chicago Blues Annual, Bay Area Music Magazine,* and the Copley news syndicate.

A personal note: I was born and raised near Clark and Fullerton, a few blocks from the Biograph Theater, when Lincoln Park was a predominantly Latino neighborhood. Growing up I played baseball, football, and softball in the vacant lot that is now a bank on the corner of Fullerton and Halsted, about one hundred yards from the rear of the Biograph. We also played cops and robbers. Many an afternoon was spent re-enacting the death of John Dillinger in the exact spot where he was shot. Old-timers in the neighborhood would point to the holes in the telephone pole in the alley, telling us these were the very bullet holes that killed Dillinger. As I grew older I realized that the large holes were used for the steel rungs the linemen inserted to climb the pole. As a child I also attended the anniversary celebration of Dillinger's shooting at the theater. We were given straw hats and a free reproduction of the famous "Dillinger Is Killed" newspaper.

LAKE CLAREMONT PRESS

Founded in 1994, **Lake Claremont Press** specializes in books on the Chicago area and its history, focusing on preserving the city's past, exploring its present environment, and cultivating a strong sense of place for the future. Visit us on the web at www.lakeclaremont.com, on Facebook, and Twitter (@ChicagoPress).

SELECTED BOOKLIST

Graveyards of Chicago

Historic Bars of Chicago

A Chicago Tavern: A Goat, a Curse, and the American Dream

Near West Side Stories: Struggles for Community in Chicago's Maxwell Street Neighborhood

Finding Your Chicago Ancestors: A Beginner's Guide to Family History in the City and Cook County

Just Add Water: Making the City of Chicago

The Beat Cop's Guide to Chicago Eats

Carless in Chicago

The Politics of Place: A History of Zoning in Chicago

What Would Jane Say? City-Building Women and a Tale of Two Chicagos

The Chicago River: A Natural and Unnatural History

The Chicago River Architecture Tour

Rule 53: Capturing Hippies, Spies, Politicians, and Murderers in an American Courtroom

For Members Only: A History and Guide to Chicago's Oldest Private Clubs

Michelle L'amour's Sexy Chicago

Hollywood on Lake Michigan: Chicago and the Movies